# *TABLE OF CONTENTS*

# Worldwide Riding Vacations

*by Arthur Sacks*

Ranches – Hotels – Point to Point – Pack Trips – Cattle Work – Safaris – Camel Rides – Endurance – Fox Hunting – Polo – Residential Learning Centers – Novice Riders to Advanced – Asia, Africa, Caribbean, The Americas, Europe, New Zealand and Australia

*Special Introduction by Bayard Fox*

First Edition

The information in this book is subject to change. The author and the publisher make no claim as to the absolute accuracy of all information. Errors and omissions may occur. Please call or write to places listed to verify and update information or look for our web address.

The Compleat Traveller
2425 Edge Hill Road
Huntingdon Valley, PA 19006
USA



ISBN 0-9653558-0-2
ISSN 1089-0394
First Edition, July, 1996
Map Graphics by Carol Cherry
Printed by Marketing Graphics
Cover by Marketing Graphics

**Cover Photos:**
**Africa** – P.J. Bestelink, Okavango Horse Safaris, Botswana
**Australia** – Australian Tourist Board
**Europe** – Exmoor Riding Holidays, England
**North America** – Horseshoe Ranch on Bloody Basin Road, Arizona

*This book is dedicated to my father,*
*who, as a recycled teenager at 92 years of age,*
*has a long history of surviving his son's*
*ventures and misadventures.*
*With all my love.*

## *FOREWORD*

pHOTO: J. BURNETT

*Arthur Sacks*

The book is about vacations. It's meant to make you smile and dream of mounting a horse and riding off into the sunset. I used lots of pictures to help ease the strain of too much reading material and to help you realize the possibility that you, too, can have a great time on horseback.

I have included destinations from some of the most enjoyable places in the world to ride; places that offer magnificent doses of natural beauty, history and culture and horses to accomplish the job. We have provided equal opportunity for English and Western riders, for novice and advanced, for families, couples and singles.

I have included an essay by Equitour owner Bayard Fox in this book. Even though I disagree with some of his views, I have included his contributions because I believe that the reader would benefit from his vast experience. Bayard has been a tireless worker in the field of promoting riding vacations and I am happy to include his generous contribution to this book.

I do not see riding holidays as a progression of harder and harder rides. Rather, I see it as an opportunity to vacation, utilizing the energy exchange between you and the horse, the environment and the cultural milieu of your chosen vacation spot. Riding vacations provide a wonderful opportunity to get outside, to get away, to use your body's energy to help you relax and feel alive.

Some people see all sporting activity as a way to compete against themselves, others or even abstract records. Others see participation in sports as a means to relax. I am from the school of relaxation. This is not to say that advanced riders, galloping along sandy beaches in Ireland or Australia, are not relaxed and having a great time. But I do not believe their experience is any more authentic then a slow paced, pack supported ride through a wilderness you never thought you would visit.

The book offers information about a variety of ways to find your dream vacation. While I offer some insight into each place listed, I presume you will want to know more details, if the place sounds attractive. Telephone numbers, fax numbers, web sites, E mail and mail addresses are provided to help you get the information. We also list several expert travel services. Some of you will choose to call those services. So mount up and enjoy!

## *ACKNOWLEDGMENTS*

This book could not have been written without professional help from the gracious crew at Marketing Graphics who helped design and print the book, with special thanks to Michael Barthe, who nursed this project home, Kathy McGee, who shaped the design, Carol Salvitty who made it flow and Erik, who gave new meaning to the expression "shake a leg." Kurt Andersen ably assisted as a proof-reader and Carol Cherry served as my resident computer wizard and contributed map graphics to the book. Thanks also go to Professor Jack Azarch, who kept saying no no to double negatives and to Sheva Stoloff for her love and patience.

Special thanks to Bayard Fox, owner of Equitour, for his fine contributions to this book. Nelly Gelich of Equitrek Australia did great work in bringing her continent alive and we appreciate it.

Finally a big thanks to you guys and gals who care for the horses and provide our readers with these wonderful opportunities to ride someone else's horses while being fed and bedded in style. The thousands of hours of work you log a week to make these vacations possible are greatly appreciated.

## *A WORD FOR NOVICES*

Beginners and the highly inexperienced riders will find lots of places and opportunities to ride around the world. Your horses will be reliable, sure-footed, "bomb-proof," gentle and easy to handle. You are not likely to encounter a situation where you will be ungraciously dumped. Finding good horses for beginners is a relatively easy task for the experienced horse people who operate the vacation destinations that appear in this book. Guest ranches and many pack supported outfitters have a good stock of horses suitable for those who want to learn. Residential learning centers are another place to learn.

The question of what vacation destination sounds best is answered in the same way as choosing non-adventure oriented travel with one major difference. Riding a horse is a physical activity, even riding one that moves at a walking pace for the duration of your ride. The tension you may bring in to the ride, the position of your legs – which may seem like they are being stretched to eternity, once you dismount – and the movement of the horse are all reasons you may feel the effects of the ride on your body. You might want to look at the description of the value of riding for the handicapped to better understand that riding is a physical activity.

Since riding is a physical activity, vacationers want to consider how much time in the saddle will be fun for them and how much recovery time they may need. I think that feeling bone weary tired from a sporting activity that is fun to do is a great feeling, a medal of honor, if you will, proudly worn and talked about around the campfire, the dining room or the lounge. But in the words of the American actor of some repute, playing a detective of ill repute, "a man must know his limits." Age need not be a concern so long as you are prepared for the after effects and you have the resources to mount and dismount a horse with or without help.

My point is don't let your heart be the only factor in choosing a vacation. Consider the needs of your body and you will have one of the most thrilling experiences possible. The exchange between the horse and rider that has fascinated humankind since time immemorial produces a wonderfully fulfilling experience. Riding vacations destinations are located in some of the most beautiful destinations imaginable. So mount up – take your family, friend or go by your little old self. Be prepared for the time of your life.

## *FOR WHAT IT'S WORTH*

The horses you find at equestrian vacation destinations are, for the most part, very well trained for their jobs. At a minimum, this means that the horses must be able to adjust to a variety of riders and their potentially inaccurate or confusing commands, created by poor balance, fear or inexperience. For those of you who wish or need to ride at a leisurely pace, you will find the horses well suited for the task. Their training and experience will help to guide you.

For those of you who like more excitement in your ride, finding the ideal horse becomes more difficult. The problems are twofold: one relating to the quality of the horse and the other to the quality of the rider. A horse that is better suited for a more advanced pace is likely to be younger and more spirited and, because he is using his athleticism to a greater degree, much more prone to injury. This makes it difficult for the supplier to always have an ideal horse ready. An older trail horse, if frightened, is likely to take a half step and shift weight slightly, hardly the stuff to knock even an inexperienced rider to the ground. A more athletic horse, when frightened, may make a five step move, dip more radically, crow hop or rear – you may get dumped.

An experienced rider may want more from a horse then he or she may be able to handle at the moment. Even so minor a discomfort as a horse who keeps throwing his head can create frustration in competent riders.

Riding vacations are therefore about finding a guide or wrangler who can listen to what you want, assess what you can accomplish and match you to the horse best suited to your ability. They may not be better riders than you, but they certainly know the horses and their abilities on what may be unfamiliar turf for you. Trust them, and things will start working out very well. If they err on the side of too much caution, changes can always be made. They are there to protect both you and their horses and the two jobs are definitely related.

# Equestrian Holidays Combine Travel and Sport

*By Bayard Fox*

I have enough faith in humanity and the course of world events to think that people will continue to turn more and more toward active, mind expanding, adventuresome holidays. There is a growing realization of the mental and physical bankruptcy of sunning on the beach and slipping coins into the slot machines at Las Vegas. People begin to seek more than an aimless, impersonal sightseeing tour by bus. The energetic and intelligent want to have an active, stimulating vacation for mind and body, pursuing a sport they enjoy, meeting new people with whom they have something in common and exposing themselves to new ideas and new ways of doing things.

This kind of holiday is for people who have a strong spirit of adventure and seek new and exciting experiences. It is for those who do not shrink from the occasional dust of the trail, patter of rain on the face or ache of tired muscles and are prepared to break with their old patterns. It is for people who are tired of glass, concrete and traffic and whose hearts leap with joy and exhilaration at the intoxicating freedom of a thundering gallop.

For those with a sense of history and a love of sports there can be no more appropriate way to travel than on horseback. This is how our ancestors, the lucky ones anyhow, used to travel. It has many advantages if one isn't just trying to get from place to place as quickly as possible, which is not really traveling at all. In parts of Europe and India, the tradition of travel on horseback was never quite lost and many of the old stables, built centuries ago, are being brought into use again. Usually there are convenient stopping places 20 or 25 miles apart where riders can easily break a journey and find accommodations for both horse and rider. People had this kind of thing in mind when these places were originally built. Some of the old rights of way going back to Roman times still exist and can be used by modern equestrians.

So often tourism has become a race from one cathedral, waterfall or canyon to another. People are transported by car or plane as quickly as possible from one sight to another. They are almost totally passive and do not participate at all in what is going on unless they are driving themselves and fighting the traffic. This kind of tourism insulates people so effectively from the places they are visiting that they might as well be watching their television sets at lesser cost. Riding tours offer travelers more physically and mentally challenging holidays which demand their active participation and bring them into close contact with the people and culture of the places they visit. On the back of a horse, one is much more a part of the country than one can be racing by in a car. Riders are not limited to the roads and see parts of the country most tourists never dream of. They have time to look unhurriedly at the country they traverse and it is easy for them to talk with people along the way. An advantage for real adventures is that people can truly get far from the beaten path.

A typical tour will last one or two weeks and riders will cover 20 to 25 miles each day, which means five or six hours in the saddle. The price for such a tour runs between $100 to $200 a day, depending on whether it is a camping trip on the old Pony Express Trail or a ride in Kenya. A hotel room in a big city can cost as much and there is no horse, guide or food thrown in. A reliable tour company will rate and compare tours which vary in the amount of skill and experience required. Some rides go at a much faster pace than others and the horses differ in tractability. No rides of this kind are for complete beginners. Riding is a sport like skiing or mountain climbing which has many degrees of attainment and cannot be safely approached at any level without adequate preparation, but an introduction is easy. The average person of almost any age who is in reasonable physical and mental shape can learn to ride in a week or two of total immersion well enough to handle some of the easier tours. On the other hand, some of the more challenging tours would require several years of experience for most people to handle with safety and enjoyment.

On the more challenging riding tours, equipment and baggage are usually moved by vehicle so that the riders can move at a varied pace with some trots and some fast gallops. It is less tiring for both people and animals to be able to vary the pace. Ring riding is a good preparation for a riding tour but many beginning riders have gotten a shock when they found how the psychology of horse and rider can change as they open up on a vast plain in Wyoming or the Hungarian puszta, on a beach in Donegal or running with the zebra in Kenya. It is of vital importance that clients find rides which are appropriate for them so that they are not bored or scared and so that they do not hold up the other members of the group.

A tour operator should offer a broad spectrum of possible choices which have been carefully tested and constantly monitored. Customer questionnaires are useful tools in keeping in touch with people's reactions to various aspects of the trips they have taken. It is extremely helpful for clients to be able to compare a number of different possibilities in making the choice which will suit them the best. An accurate understanding on the part of the client of what to expect is the best way to insure satisfaction. Sometimes, a detailed description is not enough and lengthy telephone conversations are necessary. Of course, this is only effective where the tour consultant is well informed. It is most helpful for a tour operator to ride frequently with clients to remain in close touch with their reactions and desires. The consultants must also have had broad personal experience with a number of tours to be truly effective.

No single ride can have everything, but considerations in choosing the best riding tours are the quality of the horses and tack, the food, the wine and the accommodations, the competence, friendliness and knowledge of the guides, the pace of the ride and, above all, the safety. One should look for such things as historical interest, picturesque culture, architecture, climate, music and other entertainment available to clients. It is good to avoid paved roads and noise while seeking remoteness from industrial civilization, contacts with friendly local people and opportunities to view wildlife.

A great variety of trips are possible in many countries where there is a rich horse culture and there is an abundance of contrasting opportunities. One can gallop in some of the world's best game areas with giraffe, zebra and wildebeest in Kenya's OUT OF AFRICA COUNTRY. One can follow the old Pony Express route or enjoy some of Butch Cassidy's former hideouts in Wyoming. All of these places are evocative of folklore and history to educated minds and every bit of it is inextricably entwined with horses.

The common love of things equine provides a wonderful entree everywhere and riders are greeted warmly by local people. A wonderful camaraderie usually forms quickly among the participants. The groups are usually heterogeneous and international, but they all share a fondness for horses. Most riders who travel are enterprising people who are courageous, generous of spirit, well informed, athletic and adventuresome. The stick-in-the muds, the fearful, the complacent and the narrow-minded will seldom take an equitour. Many long-term friendships are formed with people one would not otherwise have met. The number of romances which develop is amazingly high.

The aesthetic appeal of riding is enormous. The horse is an animal of such grace, power and beauty that it has fascinated mankind for millennia. Most humans have a very special relationship with horses and it is the partnership between them that made it possible to build civilization. The pleasure of a journey can be greatly enhanced by this partnership with the mount. One has the same feeling of satisfaction in sharing whatever comes with a horse that one can have with a faithful dog. Sometimes in Kenya we will have a herd of zebra cut across in front of us in an unmistakable challenge to race. The horses love this kind of stimulus. Their heads go up, their ears are pricked and their muscles tense as they accept the challenge with gusto. They can be just as fascinated with a moose in Wyoming or a blue bull in India. The necessity for this interaction between horse and rider makes the sport unique.

Horse travel usually has little impact on the environment. Horse people seek unspoiled country and tend to be well attuned to nature. Our trips through Kenya come to mind when I think about this because we often camp year after year in the same area and one can see the results. As darkness falls we tether the horses to a long rope stretched between a tree and a landrover. Manure is left here and there in the morning as we break camp, but within a few weeks it is recycled and the following year there is no sign of it except for the fact that the grass is a little greener. We do use vehicles for support, but distances are short in the average day.

For me riding day after day on a good horse creates a mood which one could never achieve by modern means of travel. When we ride across India and view those magnificent castles, walled towns, palaces and temples our sense of history is greatly enhanced through the understanding that Alexander the Great also viewed this country on horseback when he invaded the subcontinent more than 2,000 years ago. There is still no better way to see it.

Written by Bayard K. Fox, Owner
Equitour, Ltd.
PO Box 807
Dubois, WY 82513

*Bayard Fox is an inveterate horseman who has logged more than 40,000 hours in the saddle, has helped pioneer the growth of the riding vacation industry and who is a tireless worker for that industry. His love of riding comes through every line of this article and we very much appreciate his willingness to share with readers his views on riding vacations.*

# AFRICA

1 – Botswana
2 – Kenya
3 – Malawi
4 – Namibia
5 – South Africa
6 – Zimbabwe

# African Horse Safari Association

A horse safari is a unique experience for those who would combine the pleasures of long distance riding with a love for the wild and the thrill of an African safari. It is an adventure which allows you to experience African wildlife, scenery and culture at close quarters. Horse and rider become one with the environment – sharing the same sights, scents, sounds and excitement of the African wilderness. The African Horse Safari Association is a combined representation of the very best horse safaris operating in Africa. The Association sets a standard of professionalism in equine care, guiding and accommodation, combining care for the client with unrivaled personal attention to detail. Horses and tack of the best quality and traditional camping comfort of the highest standard are provided. These safaris are of a highly personalized nature and maintain their own individual character in offering a personal insight combined with a commitment to and love for the areas in which they operate.

African Horse Safari Association
36 12th Avenue, Parktown North 2193, South Africa
Tel: 27-11- 788-3923   Fax: 27 -11 880-8401

**Members**

1. Okavango Horse Safaris – Botswana
2. Offbeat Safaris – Kenya
3. Nyika Horse Safaris – Malawi
4. Reit Safari – Namibia
5. Equus Horse Safaris – South Africa
6. Carew Safaris – Zimbabwe

**Outfitter / Safaris**

## OKAVANGO HORSE SAFARIS

Privat Bag 23, Maun, Botswana
Tel: (267)-661-671 Fax: (267)-661-672
*Contact: P.J. and Barney Bestelink*

**Open March 1 through Oct.** • English tack • 18 horses • Pure Arab, American Saddle Bred, Thoroughbred, Kalahari horses, Crossbreeds • Maximum weight 210 pounds • Skill level – Fit and competent • Maximum of 10 clients • 4 to 6 hours a day riding • Children, if strong competent riders • 5 and 11 night guided safari • Traditional luxury safari tents • Hot showers en suite • Transfers from Maun airport • Member: African Horse Safari Association

The Okavango Delta's horse safari pioneers PJ and Barney Bestlelink guide you across the rolling grasslands of its flood plains, through its myriad waterways, meadows and mopane woodlands to offer you unsurpassed game viewing and birdwatching. The going is normally quite good and firm, allowing the ride to move on at a trot and canter. Game you can expect to see includes impala, buffalo, elephant, giraffe, hippopotamus, baboon, lion, cheetah and leopard. Major camp movements are supported by 4 x 4 vehicles or by mokoro (canoe), depending on water levels. Journey upriver on the Kubu Queen Houseboat and spend some days in the restful beauty of Nxamaseri Lodge at the end of safari.

PHOTO: PETER AND BEVERLY PICKFORD

**Outfitter / Safaris**

## OFFBEAT SAFARIS LIMITED

PO Box 56923, Nariobi, Kenya
Tel: (254)-2506-139 Tel: (254)-2502491 Fax: (254)-502-739
*Contact: United States Representative*

## EQUITOUR LTD. *(see page 208 and back cover)*

PO Box 807, Dubois, WY 82513, USA
Tel: 800-545-0019 Tel: 307-455-3363 Fax: 307-455-2354
E mail: equitour@Wyoming.com

**Open all year** • English tack • 35 horses • Thoroughbred, Somali horses • 14 day Endurance Rides • Combination Riding and Land Rover Safaris • Camel Safaris • Customized trips • Unexcelled game viewing • Luxury camping • Headquarters in colonial style manor house • Visits to Masai tribesmen • Member: African Horse Safari Association

The Kenya riding safari is one of Equitour's oldest and best adventures. It traverses some of the world's finest game country where riders can closely observe a tremendous quantity and variety of game from horseback. There is a close interaction with fascinating Masai tribesmen. Camping is in large and comfortable two-person tents with sheets and blankets on the beds. Hot showers and toilet facilities are convenient. Headquarters for safaris is Deloraine, the famous showplace built by Lord Francis Scott where one can stay before and after the safaris. Game viewing is also possible from land rovers and custom trips are a specialty.

**Outfitter / Safaris**

## NYIKA HORSE SAFARIS

PO Box 8, Lilongwe, Malawi, Central Africa
Tel/Fax: (265) - 740 848
*Contact: David Foot*

**Open March – Dec. 31** • Western style (McClellan saddles) • 21 Crossbreeds • Beginner to advanced riding skills • Maximum of 6 riders • 3, 5 and 10 day pack trips • 4 x 4 support vehicle • Luxury tent camps • 5 hour ride each day • Trout fishing • Vehicle safaris • Bird watching • Customized trips • Member: Safari Guides Company, African Horse Safari Association

Nyika National Park's rolling montane grasslands is unlike anywhere else in Africa. Wildlife includes eland, roan antelope, zebra, reedbuck, warthog, hyena, leopard and many others, with the possible sighting of elephants and buffalo. Our 3 to 10 night safaris (fixed dates and tailor made) are supported with pack horses or by vehicle (traditional luxury African safari camp). Escorted by a professional safari guide and an armed park scout. Bird watching, trout fishing and wildflowers. There are also vehicle safaris elsewhere in Malawi and Zambia. Founding member of African Horse Safari Association.

**Outfitter / Safaris**

## REIT SAFARI

PO Box 20706, Windhoek, Namibia
Tel: (264)-628 ask operator for Friedental 1111 Fax: (264)-61-238890
*Contact: Albert / Mrs. Waltraut Frizsche*

**Open Feb. to Oct.** • English and Western tack • 26 trail horses • Haflinger, Arabian, Lippizzaner, Trakehner, Ranch horses, Namib desert horses • 12 day trips through desert to farm coast (advanced riders only) • 6 and 7 day trips (Intermediate skilled riders welcome) • Vehicle supported • Luxury tent camps • Member: Tour and Safari Assoc. Namibia (TASA), Namibian Professional Hunters Assoc. (NAPHA), African Horse Safari Association

Reit Safari offers trails across the oldest desert in the world, the NAMIB. Riding over leopard and mountain zebra tracks from the central highland (2000 meters) to Kuiseb canyon, Welwitschia Plain, Moonvalley and the dry Swakop riverbed to Swakopmund at the shore of the Atlantic Ocean means riding through totally vast unpopulated inaccessible rock and desert landscape for 400km/9days. Or join a 350 km/11 day ride starting in Damaraland along famous rock engraving to the only place in world where elephant, rhino and giraffe live in a desert habitat. Less experienced horse lovers can join our 6 and 7 day trips. All trips are vehicle supported and are full service.

**Outfitter / Safaris**

## EQUUS HORSE SAFARIS

African Wildlife Safari on Horseback
36 12th Avenue, Parktown North 2193-WWRV
Johannesburg , South Africa
Tel: (27)-11-788-3923 Fax: (27)-11-880-8401
*Contact: Wendy Adams / Louise Montgomery*

**Open all year** • English and Trail Saddles (Western style) • Capacity 8 to 12 • 30 horses • Arabians, Friesians, Boerperde, TB Cross • Cross-country jumping • Intermediate and advanced adults and children 8 years and older • 4 to 6 hours riding daily • Outdoor plunge pool • Game and birding walks • Member: African Horse Safari Association.

Equus Horse Safaris offers the exclusive adventure of viewing Africa's big game from horseback in a private reserve of more than 50,000 acres. The reserve is host to all the major mammal species including elephant, endangered white and black rhino, buffalo, cheetah and many species of antelope. Safaris are led by experienced guides knowledgeable on the local flora and fauna. There is a friendly and relaxed atmosphere with personal service by your hosts. Horses, tack and catering are of the highest standard. Base camps safaris and wilderness pack trips are offered.

**Outfitter / Safaris**

## CAREW SAFARIS

P. Bag 295 A
Harare, Zimbabwe
Tel: (263)-58-2358 Fax: (263)-4-497746
*Contact: Geoffrey Carew*

**Open all year** • Wintec and English style • 20 horses • Thoroughbred, polo ponies, Arabians, Quarter horses • Up to 5 hours in saddle each day • Weight limit 210 if experienced • 1 to 10 day trips • Capacity 12 • Experienced skill level requirements on some trips • Stays at Kopje Tops Lodge – wilderness lodge – daily riding • Bat Caves Camp • Member: Zimbabwe Association of Tour & Safari Operators, African Horse Safari Assoc.

Zimbabwe's best Riding Safaris in the Mavuradonna Mountains. Ride with armed, professional guides on excellent horses through one of the last true wilderness areas. Track elephants, sable and other animals. Enjoy stunning views, mountains, waterfalls and bushmen painting. There are no other operators and no vehicles. All our safaris are small and tailor-made. Choose between our Tingwa Valley Safaris designed for a degree of comfort and stay at either Kopje Tops Lodge described as "remarkable, eccentric and stunningly beautiful" or ride on into Bat Caves Tented Camp, where you will encounter bucket showers and loos with views. Explorer Safaris leave the camps behind and go into the heart of the wilderness. Delicious food, fully backed-up with porters.

# ASIA

1 – India
2 – Mongolia
3 – Tibet

**Point to Point**

## ROYAL CHUKKERS

D-2, Kalindi Colony
New Delhi, 110065 India
Tel: 91-11-6919-169 Tel: 91-11-6840-037 Fax: 91-11-6822-856
*Contact: {IN U.S.} FITS EQUESTRIAN*
685 LATEEN ROAD, SOLVANG, CA 93463
Tel: 805-688-9494 Fax: 805-688-2943

**Open January through March** • English tack • 25 horses • Thoroughbreds, local "Marwari" breed, half-breds • Average time in saddle – 4 hours • 7 riding days • Ride across country • Every night in a different place along the way (forts, castles, luxury tents, feudal home, etc.) • Capacity 16 riders

Our ride is in Rajasthan, which, prior to 1947, consisted of several royal kingdoms. The rulers governed through local feudal lords in whose magical residences we spend the night after a long day's ride. Terrain unique to Rajasthan is the Thar Desert and the Aravalli range. Our ride is through the fringes of the desert to more fertile areas scattered with lakes and forests around the Aravallis. Horses used are thoroughbreds, the native "Marwaris" and half-breds. The tack is English. Meals are sumptuous and evenings offer entertainment by local entertainers and musicians giving an insight into the life style of the native people.

**Outfitter**

## BOOJUM EXPEDITION

14543 Kelly Canyon Road
Bozeman, Montana 59715, USA
Tel: 406-587-0125 Fax: 406-585-3474 E-Mail: boojum@mcn.net
http: //www.manymedia.com/tibet/Boojum.html
*Contact: Kent Madin*

**June to September** • Russian cavalry saddles, traditional saddles • 19 day trip • 7 to 9 day wilderness packing by horse • 15 to 25 miles per day • Native horses • All skill levels • 9 to 10 days sightseeing Ulaan Baatar, Mongolian countryside • Children on case by case basis • 14 Rider limit

Our riding area is Hovsgol, near the Siberian border, one flight and two days drive from the capitol Ulaan Baatar. We cover a variety of terrain traveling through open valleys dotted with tent-like gers, dense larch forests and rocky passes above the tree line. Clear rivers, great fishing and tall mountains are all part of this landscape reminiscent of Montana 100 years ago. Highlights include the traditional Naadam festival with archery, wrestling and horse races. We visit the summer camp of the "reindeer people" who raise milk and RIDE! reindeer. Be prepared to try fermented mare's milk, the traditional libation during summer in Mongolia.

**Outfitter**

## BOOJUM EXPEDITIONS

14543 Kelly Canyon Road
Bozeman, Montana 59715, USA
Tel: 406-587-0125 Fax: 406-585-3474 E-Mail: boojum@mcn.net
http: //www.manymedia.com/tibet/Boojum.html
*Contact: Kent Madin*

**June to September** • Russian cavalry saddles, traditional saddles • 19 day trip • 7 to 9 day wilderness packing by horse • 15 to 25 miles per day • Native horses • All skill levels • 10 days sightseeing in Beijing, Chengdu, Hong Kong, Sichuan countryside • Children on case by case basis • 14 Rider limit •

Our ride takes place at 11,000 feet on the wild flower covered plateau of eastern Tibet between the Yangtze and Yellow rivers. In the distance, 20,000 foot peaks rim the horizon and prayer flags flutter on nearby hillsides. We ride for seven days among the "black tent" nomads: yak and sheep herders, devout Tibetan Buddhists and superb horsemen. We'll see large and small Buddhist temples and meet nomad families as they move their stock to new pastures. This is a ride back in time in a culture that is little changed in centuries. Traveling to and from the riding area we visit Beijing, Chengdu and Hong Kong.

# Australia and New Zealand

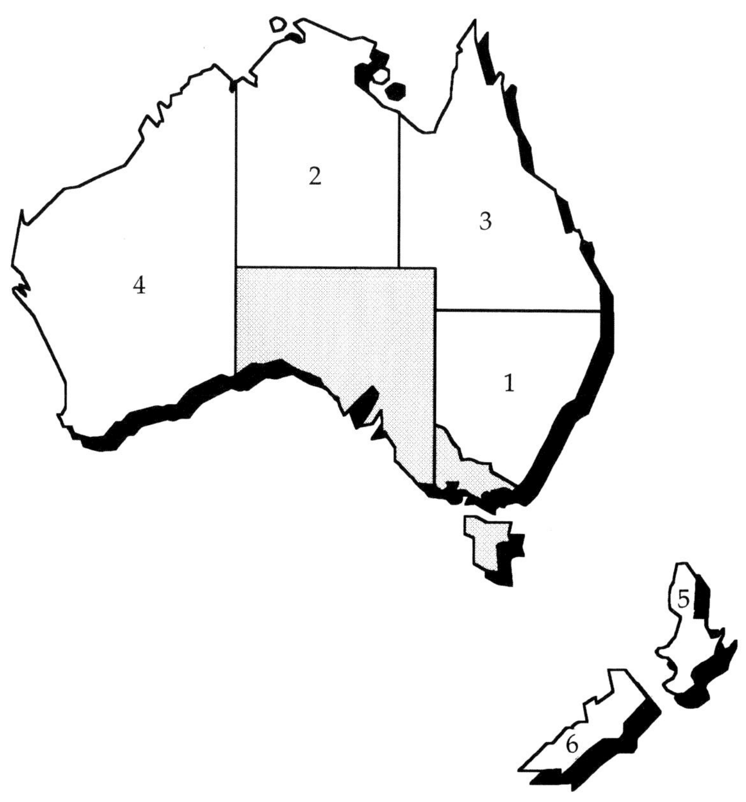


1 – New South Wales
2 – Northern Territory
3 – Queensland
4 – Western Australia
5 – New Zealand, North Island
6 – New Zealand, South Island

# Australia

That wonderful multifarious land down under. Men on their horses blazed the trails which later became our highways, took cattle to far off places which later became cities, founded the route for the overland telegraph which then linked the south to the north and so reduced the "tyranny of distance." Horses are part of us.

You can ride the savannas of the far Northwest and be part of a cattle muster on a 2 million acre ranch or "station," as it's called down under. You can ride through the tropical rain forest from the table land to the coast below. You can ride with our endurance champions on their competition horses, so fit they fairly burst, so expertly and lovingly handled that they are ridden in rope halters at a cracking pace through forested hills and open plains. You can ride in the mighty Snowy Mountains on the country that the "Man from the Snowy River" rode. You can ride through the Karri forests of the Southwest and emerge on deserted beaches welcoming the breakers from the Indian Ocean. There is not much you can't do! You can sleep in a swag, a tent, a shearers hut, a country pub or a four poster in a grand homestead. You will ride good, reliable sure-footed horses, many of them descendants from the famous Walers which supplied many armies for nearly a century.

Although our accent may differ from others, English speakers are understood. We forgive you for not using all of our expressions like swag, billy and the station and hope you forgive us for our dry sense of humor on the driest continent on earth. What you probably don't expect is the bustling modern cities: Sydney with its beautiful harbor, bay and inlets; elegant, stately, fashionable Melbourne; beautiful, easy going Brisbane; Perth, a city closer to Singapore than to the Eastern capitals; multicultural, tropical Darwin; Cairns and who could forget "The Alice," a transit centre leading to nowhere, on a river with no water that sponsors an annual regatta where the flow of beer far exceeds the flow of the River Todd.

That's what we offer and enjoy sharing with you. How about it? When Aussies say "G' Day" they mean it. Come have a good day yourself.

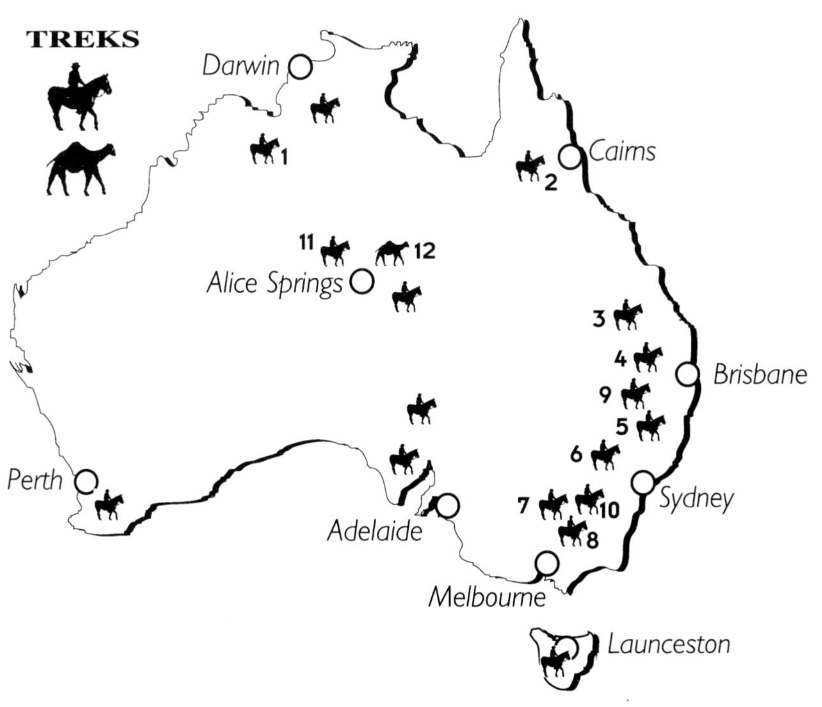
TREKS
Darwin
1
Cairns
2
11
12
Alice Springs
3
4
Brisbane
9
5
6
Perth
Sydney
7
10
8
Adelaide
Melbourne
Launceston

# Yes! Next Holiday... Equitrek Australia

Your Sydney based travel service has the experience and facility to co-ordinate the best riding adventures Australia wide.

Novice to experienced riders, teens to "seens," 5 star comfort seekers to camping aficionados.

Rides, farmstays and learning vacations in all equestrian disciplines year round.

Whatever you want to do in Australia, we are here to help you do it in the best possible way!

We can help plan your golf, sailing, snorkeling, scuba diving, swimming, tennis, bushwalking, white water rafting, parasailing, whale watching, gliding, abseiling, 4WD touring and eco drives while you are visiting.

We can even arrange a night at the Sydney opera.

**EQUITREK AUSTRALIA**
5 King Road, Ingleside NSW 2101
Tel: (61)-2-9913-9408 Fax: (61)-2-9970-6303
E Mail: equitrek@magna.com.au
Web Page: http://www.equineoz.com.au/equitrek
*Contact: Nelly Gelich*

Open all year. Many diverse venues. Rides from 1 day to 2 weeks. Mainly Australian stock horses. Tack is Australian stock saddles (very comfortable), English and some Western. Camp-out to accommodated rides; facilities from basic to 5 star. Catering from novice to experienced riders.

*See Color Photo Page 116*

**Point to Point / Inn to Inn / Sydney area to Port Macqurie**

## KELLY'S BUSHRANGING ADVENTURES

The Ridgeway, Kendall, NSW 2439
Tel: (61)-65-594-478 Fax: (61)-65-569-682
*Contact: Peter / Caroline or*

## EQUITREK AUSTRALIA

5 King Road, Ingleside, NSW 2101, Australia
E mail: equitrek@magna.com.au
Tel: (61)-2-9913-9408 Fax: (61)-2-9970-6303
*Contact: Nelly*

**Open all year** • English and Australian tack • Arabian endurance trained horses • 2 to 6 day inn to inn style • Customized trips by arrangement • Skill level – fit and competent • Guest capacity 6 • Swimming in season • Average saddle time 6 hours • Climate cool to hot • Meeting point – Kendall (Port Macqurie area)

Gourmet quality food, well trained endurance bred Arabians and high quality accommodations characterize Peter Kelly's Bushranging Adventures. On the two and three day gourmet rides you stay in secluded, luxury farmhouses, enjoy quality creekside picnics, savour the lush green beauty of the rainforest trails, ocean views, mountain lookouts, long trots and canters on extremely fit and responsive horses. Your host and guide, Peter, has great knowledge and love of the area and is well qualified to look after you. On our 4 to 7 day treks we utilize quality bed and breakfasts. All meals are provided and luggage is transferred. Special programs by arrangement include riding on deserted North Coast beaches. Non-riders welcome.

*Map Reference 5*

**Point to point / Camping**

## KHANCOBAN TRAIL RIDES

PO Box 91, Khancoban, NSW 2642
Tel/Fax: (61)-60-76-9455
*Contact: John / Jackie Williams or*

## EQUITREK AUSTRALIA

5 King Road, Ingleside, NSW 2101, Australia
E mail: equitrek@magna.com.au
Tel: (61)-2-9913-9408 Fax: (61)-2-9970-6303
*Contact: Nelly*

**Open Oct. to May** • Australian stock saddles • 30 Australian stock horses • 3 to 5 day camping trips • Vehicle supported or pack • Accommodations arranged on request • Guest capacity 12 • Average saddle time 7 hours • Intermediate skill level required • Trout fishing available • Climate – alpine cold to hot • Meeting point – Cooma

Based at "Tom Groggin" Station, you retrace the trails and use campsites of "The Man from Snowy River." As you look down that terrible descent, you thank the lucky stars that you don't have to ride it and wonder how on earth they did, 101 years ago. The superb scenery is still there and so are the river, the brumbies, kangaroos, emus and the snow gums. The courageous spirit of the mountain horse still flows in the veins of your mount who was trained with care to be a most agreeable and safe partner. John or Jackie will happily answer all your questions about "The Man" as you ride along. You have the choice of joining a vehicle back-up ride, a total packhorse trip or stay at the station and go for day rides.

*Map Reference 8*

**Point to Point / Inn to Inn**

## SNOWY RIVER HORSEBACK ADVENTURE

PO Box 77, Cooma, NSW 2630
Tel: (61)-64-537260 Fax: (61)-64-537-251
*Contact: Annemarie Verspae*

**Open Oct. through May** • Australian stock saddles • 25 horses • Australian stock horse, Anglo-Arabian, Thoroughbred • All skill levels • 2, 3 and 5 day lodge to lodge trips • 6 hours in saddle each day • Capacity 12 riders • On 5 day trip indoor pool and spa • Fishing • Meeting point – Cooma

Riding the Man From Snowy River Country in Style. We take small groups on 2, 3 and 5 day horse riding treks through the most picturesque Snowy Mountain high country, on the southern side of Jindabyne, N.S.W. This horse riding vacation successfully combines adventure with comfort. Instead of sleeping out at night, riders arrive at the end of each exhilarating day in the saddle at a comfortable lodge/guesthouse in picturesque bushland with mountain and lake front settings, to be treated to excellent three course meals and Aussie country hospitality at its best. The emphasis is kept on personal touch, gourmet food, superb and varying scenery, comfort, quality horses and equipment and wildlife.

*Map Reference 10*

**Point to point / Inn to Inn**

## STEVE LANGLEY / PUB CRAWLS ON HORSEBACK

Bullock Mountain Homestead, Box WWRV
Glen Innes, NSW 2370, Australia
Tel: (61)-67-321599 Fax: (61)-67-323538
*Contact: Steve Langley*

**Open all year** • Australian stock saddles • 30 Australian stock horses • Intermediate skill level • Children who ride are welcome • 3, 5, 6 and 10 day trips • On 10 day trips, some camp outs (experienced and fit riders) • 5 to 6 hours riding daily • Lessons available • Fishing • Guest Capacity of 24 • Meeting point – Glen Innes

Australia's only continuous **pub to pub ride,** staying in different historical old bush pubs. Each night enjoy a 3 course candlelight dinner, log fire and comfy beds. Wake up to cooked country breakfasts. Six day "Great Aussie" Pub Crawl averages 35 kilometers a day of magnificent NSW High Country, with a day of rest and vehicle excursion into wilderness country, topped by an old fashioned Aussie bush BBQ. **"Ride the Divide"** is an exciting 10 day August ride over the Great Dividing Range and along the coastline. The ride combines pub stays and camp out. Experienced and capable riders only. Ride covers approximately 260 kilometers.

*Map Reference 9*

**Point to Point / Camping**

## TALBINGO TRAILS

3 Troon Place, Pymble, NSW 2073
Tel: (61)-2-440-8775 Fax: (61)-2-440-8903
*Contact: Kerry Shanley or*

## EQUITREK AUSTRALIA

5 King Road, Ingleside, NSW 2101, Australia
E mail: equitrek@magna.com.au
Tel: (61)-2 -9913-9408 Fax: (61)-2-9970-6303
*Contact: Nelly*

**Open Oct. to May** • Australian stock saddle • 20 Australian stock horses • 3 to 5 day camping trips, either vehicle supported or pack • Average saddle time 7 hours • Intermediate skill level required • Luxury style accommodation arranged on request • Climate alpine cold to hot • Trout fishing available • Meeting point – Cooma

Sylvia and Everett Oldfield, descendants of Snowy pioneers, know their country, their horses, the Snowy traditions and how to produce the best food on the open fire. Kangaroos and brumbies show some interest in you, and if you don't have a spare roll of film on hand, you'll regret it. Most of the riding is done in the Kosciusko National Park. You encounter steep mountain sides, open high plain grazing country, carpets of alpine flowers and tall Mountain Ash offering shade and a perfect ride. The pace is adjusted to the terrain and your ability. The luxury accommodation version of this adventure is available offering trout fishing and the rare opportunity to watch platypus play in the river.

*Map Reference 7*

**Point to Point / Pack horse trips**

## WILDERNESS RIDES

"Bora" Enmore, via Uralla, NSW 2358
Tel/Fax: (61)-67-782-172
*Contact: Max / Arleen Brennan or*

## EQUITREK AUSTRALIA

5 King Road, Ingleside, NSW 2101, Australia
E mail: equitrek@magna.com.au
Tel: (61)-2-9913-9408 Fax: (61)-2-9970-6303
*Contact: Nelly*

**Open Sept. to June** • 30 horses • Australian stock and Arabians • Australian tack • 3 and 5 day pack trips • Average time in saddle 6 hours • Intermediate skill level • Swimming in season • Tents, bedding, meals supplied • Extremely steep descents • Climate cold to hot • Meeting Point – Armidale

Wilderness Rides specializes in pack horse adventures into the spectacular New England gorges. This country is only accessible on horseback. The gorges drop dramatically away – 500 meters – with spectacular views. The carefully managed area has a large variety of fauna and flora including rare rock wallabies, wallaroos, ancient trees, numerous birds, flowers, swimming holes and natural spa baths. Camping under the stars and awakening to the dawn chorus of birds have universal appeal. Max, your host, is third generation of his family to run some cattle in the gorges. One suspects his horses to have a touch of mountain goat in their genes. Their rock negotiation skills are unsurpassed.

*Those of you who don't have a head for heights – beware.*

*Map Reference 6*

**Camel Safari**

## FRONTIER CAMEL TOURS P/L

PO Box 2836M Alice Springs, N.T. 0871, Australia
Tel: (61)-8-89-530-444 Fax: (61)-8-89-555015
*Contact: Michelle Smail or*

## EQUITREK AUSTRALIA

5 King Rd, Ingleside NSW 2101, Australia
E mail: equitrek@magna.com.au
Tel: (61)-2-9913-9408 Fax: (61)-2-9970-6303 or
*Contact: Nelly*

**Open April through Oct.** • 1, 3 and 6 day camel safaris • Customized camel safaris • Previous riding experience unnecessary • Good standard fitness required • Camel riding lessons included • Large variation in climate • Minimum safari size is 4 • Maximum is 10 people on 1 day ride – 8 people on 3 day ride – 7 people on 6 day ride • Departures from Alice Springs

Traveling at a camel's pace in Central Australia brings visitors closer to the unspoiled nature and vastness of this dry land... no crowds – no traffic! Enjoy huge horizons, beautiful landscapes, special flora and fauna from atop our fit, well trained, highly sociable camels. The 3 day Western MacDonnell Safari leads through sandy riverbeds and ancient rocky ridges. Camp 1 night, enjoy Glen Helen Gorge accommodations 1 night. Experience the Simpson Desert and Chambers Pillar on the 6 day safari. Enjoy red sand dunes and camping under the stars in swags, savory camp oven meals and the hospitality of Maryvale homestead on the last day.

*Map Reference 11*

**Point to point / Camp-outs / Day Rides**

## OSSIE'S OUTBACK HORSE TREKS

18 Warburton St., Alice Springs, N.T. 0870
Tel: (61)-8-8952-2308 Fax: (61)-8-8952-2211
*Contact: Harry / Sandy Osborn or*

## EQUITREK AUSTRALIA

5 King Rd, Ingleside NSW 2101, Australia
E mail: equitrek@magna.com.au
Tel: (61)-2-9913-9408 Fax: (61)-2-9970-6303 or
*Contact: Nelly*

**Open all year** • Australian tack • 15 Australian stock horses • Half day and all day rides • 3 and 5 day customized treks • All skill levels • Average riding time 3 to 6 hours a day • Large variation in climate • Budget type accommodations available at base • Meeting point – Alice Springs

We offer Outback horse riding at its best on our fit and sure-footed stock horses. Enjoy unique adventures "in the spirit of the explorers and stockmen" and the outback's spectacular and varied landscape. Although wildlife sightings are common, sometimes the marsupials have a day off. For Alice Springs visitors our daily 4 hour rides include Nature Trail, Heritage Trail, Sunset Night Ride and Gourmet Bush Picnic. Our all day rides, popular from April to October, allow you to experience the remoteness of Red Centre and enjoy a BBQ lunch and Billy tea. Our 3 to 5 day customized treks take us into the remote Western MacDonnell Ranges in the manner of our pioneers.

*Map Reference 12*

Guest Ranch

## HORSE TREK AUSTRALIA

Horse Trek Australia, PO Box 625, Maleny Q 4552
Tel: (61)-74-460-936 Fax: (61)-74-460-755
*Contact: Bob Sample or*

## EQUITREK AUSTRALIA

5 King Road, Ingleside, NSW 2101, Australia
E mail: equitrek@magna.com.au
Tel: (61)-2-9913-9408 Fax: (61)-2-9970-6303
*Contact: Nelly*

**Open all year** • Australian stock endurance saddles • 20 horses • Arabian crossbred • Climate warm to hot • Scheduled 7 day monthly treks – 7 hours each day • Intermediate skill levels required • Guest capacity of 12 • Swimming • Sauna • Hot tub • Meeting point – Brisbane area

Host farm is nestled in the charming hills of Sunshine Coast hinterland, 80 km. north of Brisbane. We offer quality horses, comfortable accommodations, home cooked meals and wonderful trails leading through rain forests, hoop pine and eucalyptus forests. You'll see kangaroos, wallabies, many parrots, possibly koalas. Hosts/guides are champion endurance riders with many wins. They breed, rear and train responsive, athletic Anglo-Arabian horses. Horses are selected to suit your ability and confidence... 200 kilometers of scenic, challenging, yet always safe trails. Our night ride, fast runs and small groups make for a unique riding experience. Rides are farm based, using different trails. Daily-lunches from saddlebag. Entertaining program for non-riders.

*Map Reference 4*

**Guest Ranch / Point to Point / Cattle Drives**

## KROOMBIT TOURIST PARK

Kroombit Tourist Park, "Lochenbar" PO Box 135, Biloela, Q 4715
Tel: (61)-79-922-186 Fax: (61)-79-924-186
*Contact : Alan or Carol Sandilands or*

## EQUITREK AUSTRALIA

5 King Road, Ingleside, NSW 2101, Australia
E mail: equitrek@magna.com.au
Tel: (61)-2-9913-9408 Fax: (61)-2-9970-6303
*Contact: Nelly*

*See Color Page 116*

**Open all year** • 40 Australian stock horses • Australian tack • 3 and 5 day trips or farmstay rides • Average time in saddle 6 hours • Novice to intermediate skill level • Swimming • Self catering air conditioned cabins and camping facilities available or full board packages • Climate warm to hot • Meeting point – Bileola

The 10,000 acre Kroombit Tourist Park is 580 kilometers north of Brisbane. It enjoys beautiful weather and is built on a 10,000 acre working cattle property. All horses are good, reliable working stock horses and know their job. We are located along a beautiful part of Australia's National Trail. You can holiday in cabins or pitch your own tent, self cater or join us. We offer 3 or 5 day treks, rides from base or tag along on a cattle drive. 4 Wheel Drive tours are available. Swim, do a Clydesdale drawn wagon ride or just muck around and enjoy yourself watching the local wildlife. Having a good time is easy at this great spot where the Outback bids you a friendly "Good-Day"...

*Map Reference 3*

**Point to Point / Camping**

## MOUNT MOLLOY TRAIL RIDES

Little Road, Mt. Molloy, Q 4871
Tel: (61)-70-94-1382 Fax: (61)-2-9970-6303
*Contact: Peter / Heather Brown or*

## EQUITREK AUSTRALIA

5 King Road, Ingleside, NSW 2101, Australia
E mail: equitrek@magna.com.au
Tel: (61)-2-9913-9408 Fax: (61)-2-9970-6303
*Contact: Nelly*

**Open Feb. to Nov.** • Australian tack • 30 Australian stock horses • 2, 4 and 6 day trips • 4WD back up • Tents and all meals supplied • Guest capacity of 12 • Intermediate skill level • Average saddle time – 6 hours • Full service vehicle supported • River swimming • Climate tropical warm to hot • Meeting Point – Port Douglas (90 km. north of Cairns)

The treks start just outside Port Douglas in the coastal cane fields, then abruptly and very steeply climb into the rain forest and from there to grazing country and open forests of the table lands. Waterfalls, deserted mines, a bat colony, outback pubs, campsites by billabongs and creeks where you can swim with your horse are all part of this unique experience. The horses are friendly and ideally conditioned for the climate and the work they perform. You will learn to play a didgeridoo during the evenings by the campfire, maybe even learn how to cook a damper. It is a beautiful, leisurely ride making the most of the tropical ambiance of Far North Queensland.

*Map Reference 2*

**Point to Point / Camping**

## KIMBERLY PURSUITS

PO Box 5, Wyndham, WA 6740
Tel: (61)-91-611-029 Fax: (61)-2-9970-6303
*Contact: Roderick Woodland or*

## EQUITREK AUSTRALIA

5 King Road, Ingleside, NSW 2101, Australia
E mail: equitrek@magna.com.au
Tel: (61)-2-9913-9408 Fax: (61)-2-9970-6303
*Contact: Nelly*

**Open May to September** • English, Western and Australian stock saddles • 50 horses • Thoroughbreds, Australian stock horses • 4WD supplied camp out rides • 2, 4, 7 and 11 day trips • Intermediate skill required • Average saddle time 7 hours • Group capacity 10 • One cattle round-up • Advanced riding skills • River swimming • Fishing • Temperatures average 32C (85F), no rain • Meeting point – Wyndham (100 km north of Kununurra)

The remote Kimberly region is Australia's Wild West. Stunning gorges, golden plains and valleys following mesas, magic waterholes and thermal springs on a **million acre farm** are yours to enjoy. The bizarre shaped Boab trees add magic to fiery sunsets. Experience wild horses, flocks of cockatoos, brolgas and maybe even a crocodile. Campfire fare and tales and sleeping in the swag add new meaning to "going bush." Your host, Roderick, expertly ensures your enjoyment. Horses are surefooted and well suited for their environment. On longer rides horses run along loose so they can carry riders every second day. The Equitrek add-on program visiting the unique Bungle Bungle mountains by small charter aircraft is highly recommended.

*Map Reference 1*

# New Zealand

Yes, folks, New Zealand is a country. I know it's somewhere near Australia but I'm not quite sure where. I know it has a lot of sheep – the jokes abound. It grows a lot of kiwis which are some kind of New Age fruit that has been appearing in all of the upscale restaurants worldwide.

*BUT*

Did you know that New Zealand is divided into two distinct island groups, North and South Islands? That New Zealand is a land of incredible green beauty, rolling hills, rugged snow covered mountains, charming cities, thousands of miles of beachfront, a temperate climate at all but the higher altitudes and a genuine native people, the Maoris, who have not only not been wiped out but who own and operate some of the rides offered?

The horse is a natural addition to the New Zealand climate and topography and all types of equestrian sports abound. Our riding packages are varied from stays at self catering cottages to longer treks on English and Western saddles, from mountain riding to beach riding.

And don't forget our great golf courses, wonderful fishing, great hiking trails and more. So come on down to our friendly environment, spend a week or a month – you will not regret it.

**Point to Point / Stationary**

## PAKIRI BEACH HORSE RIDES AND OVERNIGHT SAFARIS LTD.

2 R.D., Wellsford, New Zealand
Tel/Fax: (64)-9-422-6275
*Contact: Sharley / Laly Haddon*

**Open all year** • English and Western, Stock • 70 horses • Appaloosa, Arabian, Quarter, Mixed breed • Half and all day rides • Full service farm stays • Self catering • 2 to 4 day treks – camping style to executive lodges – customized • All skill levels • Fishing • Hiking • Canoeing • Birdwatching • Guest capacity of 6 • 1-1/2 hours from Auckland city

Pakiri is a genuine New Zealand farm hosted by descendants of the area's first Maori rangitira (chief). We offer riding holidays and breed Arabians and Thoroughbreds. Riding programs include 1 and 2 hour rides along the beach and through the dunes to half day, full day and multi day safaris over green sheep and cattle farmland, through native New Zealand bush, along the unpopulated white sand Pacific surf beach and through exotic pine forests. We follow old coach trails and ancient Maori tracks. You can stay in comfortable, equipped tents on the beach, in native tipi, shearers quarters, beach cabins or a beautifully appointed executive lodge. We offer a variety of high quality meal plans.

**Point to Point**

## TE UREWERA ADVENTURES

Ruatahuna, Private Bag 3001, Rotorua, New Zealand
Tel: (64)-7-366-3969 Fax: (64)-7-366-3333
*Contact: Margaret Biddle*

**Open all year** • Stock saddles • 30 horses • 1 to 5 day riding programs, camping and some B&B opportunities, customized packages • Fishing from the back of horseback – trips can be arranged • Swimming in season • Marae visits and sleeping quarters

Tucked away in the central North Island is Te Urewara National Park, the home of the Tuhoe people. Riding with us is a ride through our beautiful wilderness and a ride through the history of the Maori people. Come and share the hospitality of this Maori tribe. Experience a ride through rugged untouched landscape, molded by the great forces of nature – its many charms and myths kept alive by these people, the "Children of the Mist." Visit a Maori village, learn the customs, the culture and history and enjoy the hospitality of your hosts Margaret and Whare Biddle. Taste a Maori hangi – food cooked in the ground – in this unique "once in a lifetime experience."

**Guest Ranch / Cattle Drives / Point to Point**

## WHANANAKI TRAIL RIDES

Redburn Farms via Whananaki Beach Store
Whananaki, Northland, New Zealand
Tel: (64)-9-433-8299 Tel: (64)-25-949-437(Mobile)
Fax: (64)-9-433-8286
*Contact: Stewart McKenzie-Pollock*

**Open all year** • English, western and stock saddles • 23 horses • Appaloosa, Arabians and Quarter horses • All skill levels • Daily trail riding • Cattle mustering • Rodeo • Team penning • Dressage training • Overnight campouts • 2 to 6 day treks – campouts • Extended treks • Stay at old Kauri house on property • Stays at modern farmhouse • Wind surfing • Kayaking • Deep sea fishing • Transfers from Whangarei and Auckland airports

The Trail Ride Centre is on a 730 acre beef ranch located on the east coast of the North Island. The ranch breeds several breeds of cattle. There is daily horse riding. Accommodation arrangements are an old kauri house without electricity, camper van sites or guests at the main farm house. Horse treks are by arrangement. These include two day rides, camping out overnight and cooking on an open fire. On the five day treks, cabins are available. These treks can go 100 kilometers away from civilization and traffic into Russell State Forest. For people not interested in horses there are bush walks, beaches and deep sea fishing. This far out in the country, there is no need to rush and the hospitality is outstanding.

Farmhouse

## KOWHAI EQUESTRIAN FARM STAY

Island Road, View Hill, Oxford, 8253, Canterbury
Tel: (64)-3-312-4309 Tel: (64)-25-366-826 Fax: (64)-3-312-3079
*Contact: Liz / Chris Thomas*

**Open all year** • English riding • 65 horses • Thoroughbreds, Arabians, New Zealand Warm Bloods • Lessons – dressage, cross-country and show jumping • Trekking • Children welcome • Capacity 8 • Farm Stay or 27 in bunkhouse by arrangement • Beginner to advanced

Kowhai is situated at the base of the Southern Alps on a picturesque, privately owned estate just 45 minutes from Christchurch, in the South Island of New Zealand. Kowhai has been operating for 26 years. Guests are welcome to stay any length of time from a 2 hour trek to a 3 month farm stay. We offer return transportation from Christchurch (airport or accommodation). Farm stay accommodation – private double or twin rooms, all meals, horse riding and quality instruction. Many beautiful treks through hills and native bush from 2 hours to full day. Also available – fishing and shooting.

**Point to point / Camping + Basic Mt. Huts**

## NEW ZEALAND BACKCOUNTRY SADDLE EXPEDITION

RD 1, Cardrona Valley, Wanaka, Otago, New Zealand
Tel: (64)-3-443-815 Fax: (64)-3-443-1712
*Contact: Debbie Thompson*

**Open all year** • Western tack • 30 horses • Appaloosa and Some Standardbred • 2 hour rides, several 3 and 4 day pack trips • 6 hours average time in saddle • Hunting trips in season • Horses for all skill levels • Good fishing opportunities • Guest capacity on overnights 8 people • 35 km from Queenstown

In the South Island of New Zealand, 27 km from Lake Wanaka in the Cardrona Valley, are the stables of New Zealand's Backcountry Saddle Expeditions. The stables operate in all seasons, 2 hour rides being the most popular. For the more serious rider, all day and overnight rides are available during our summer months. Our Appaloosa horses with Western saddles provide the safest and most comfortable ride for trekkers. Safety helmets and waterproof clothing are provided where necessary. All pack trips are backed up by pack horses and accommodation is in huts. The views are stunning with long vistas and snow-capped mountains. The terrain can be challenging and the experience of nature is unforgettable.

**Self Catering Holiday Homes / Point to Point**

## WESTERN RANGES HORSE TREKS

Baton Valley, Wakefield RD 2, New Zealand
Tel: (64)-3-5433864 Tel: (64)-3-5224178 Fax: (64)-3-5433860
*Contact: Dion MacLean*

**Open all year** • English tack • 14 horses • Hunters, Welsh cobs, Quarter, Arabian • 1 to 3 day based treks North-West Nelson Range • All skill levels • Muster sheep and cattle • 5 hours per day riding • 5 to 10 guest capacity • Cross-country course • Swim horses in river • Swimming • Fishing • Nearby rafting – kayaking

# Caribbean and Central and South America

1 – Dominican Republic
2 – Jamaica
3 – Belize
4 – Costa Rica
5 – Mexico
6 – Ecuador

Resort

## CASA DE CAMPO

La Romana, Dominican Republic
Tel: 800-877-3643 Tel: 305-856-5405 Fax: 305-858-4677
*Contact: Local travel agent or Premier World Marketing*

**Open all year** • English-Western saddles • Hundreds of horses • Trail riding • Jumping • Polo • All skill levels • Lessons • 300 Rooms – 150 Villa Homes • 2 golf courses • 14 tennis courts • Shooting center • Pools • Beaches • Sailing • Deep water fishing • Fitness and health center • 9 restaurants • Special children's program

Enjoy Casa de Campo's comforts with luxury casita rooms or private villa homes perfect for family and friends. Riders and non riders can enjoy a host of Caribbean activities including golf on our two world famous Peter Dye designed golf courses and wonderful Caribbean and international meals at a variety of restaurants. A complete children's program makes us a family paradise. Our very diversified riding program includes exciting beach and inland trail riding for all skill levels, world class polo, jumping courses and lessons. All inclusive packages include unlimited trail riding, tennis, all meals, accommodations, drinks and more. Guests can jet directly to Casa de Campo (LRM) on American Airlines.

*See Color Photo Page 117*

**Residential Riding Centre**

## CHUKKA COVE FARM, LTD.

PO Box 160, Ocho Rios
St. Ann, Jamaica, West Indies
Tel: 809-972-2506 Fax: 809-972-0814
*Contact: Reservations*

**Open year round** • English tack • 42 Horses • Thoroughbreds, Anglo-Arab and Quarter horses • 1 hour tour of Chukka Cove, 2 hour ride to village of Chester in mountains, 3 hour rides to beach – swim with your horse and 6 hour swim – horse trek rides • Overnight trek rides • Polo lessons • Riding lessons • Jumping lessons • Children 8 and older • Pony rides for little ones • Helmets supplied

Chukka Cove Farm, Ltd. is full service residential riding centre. The centre provides the highest quality horses and tack and offers riding opportunities for all skill levels. Lessons are recommended for all beginners and treks into mountains are restricted to experienced riders who can handle their horses at all gaits and in varied terrain. Breeches and high boots are preferred but western dress is suitable. There are 3 hour rides to the beach where you can unsaddle and swim your horse, a two hour ride through working farms to the mountain village of Chester as well as overnight treks to Lillyfield Great House.

**Resort / Jungle Treks**

## BANANA BANK LODGE

PO Box 48, Belmopan, Belize
Tel/Fax: 501-8-12020 E mail: bbl@bcsl.com.bz
*Contact: John Meith*

**Open all year** • Western tack • 25 horses • Quarter horse types • Trail riding • Customized 1/2, full day and up to 7 day excursions into the bush (camping option, weather permitting) • Guest capacity 35 • 2 Bedroom cabanas • Swimming in river • Canoeing • Birdwatching • Hiking • English and Spanish spoken • Transfers from Belize City, taxi or bus to property

Explore the tropical jungles of Belize by horseback. The temperature is 80 degree at least 350 days a year. Located on the Belize River, there are birds, tropical wild life and our own unexcavated Maya ruins. Design your own equestrian vacation with half-day, full day or even week long excursions into the bush (camping option, weather permitting). Western tack with fast or slow responsive, well trained horses. Non-riding day trip options are available. Hearty American and Belizean meals are served family style in our thatched roof restaurant. Our comfortable 2 bedroom cabanas in quiet garden settings are ideal for families or small groups.

**Country Hotels**

*"WELCOME TO COSTA RICA RIDE"*

## VESA TOURS

PO Box 476-239-1049, Ciudad Cariari – San Jose, Costa Rica
Tel: (506)-239-1049 Tel: (506)-239-0328 Fax: (506)-293-4206
*Contact: Vesa Tours*

**Open all year** • Costa Rican saddles • Criollos • Average saddle time each day – 2 to 6 hours • Intermediate skill level • 8 nights, 9 days with option for 5 day beach extension • Accommodations with private bath, hot water • Stays at Fonda Vela, Chachagua Rain Forest Hotel and Pacuare Lodge • Swimming • White water rafting • Transfers supplied • Tours are conducted in English • Member: WORLDWIDE ORGANIZATION OF EQUESTRIAN TOURISM

Join us for a 10 day tour in a tropical paradise – Costa Rica! We feature horseback riding in three distinct areas of the country. You'll ride through tropical rain forests and lush cloud forests on outings to scenic views of waterfalls and active volcanoes! And at the third destination you will go rafting down a wild and scenic river to get to your overnight accommodations and awaiting mounts. Try toping that for adventure and excitement. Enjoy delicious food and comfortable lodging at excellent quality hotels. Plenty of additional activities for non-riders and riders alike. Please contact us for complete details about your next riding vacation.

PHOTO: FONDA VELA PROPERTY

**Guest Ranch**

## RANCHO MADRONO

Apartado 46, Patzcuaro, Michoacan, Mexico 61600
Tel: (52)-431-8-19-41 Fax: (52)-434-2-33-95
*Contact: Tom V. Roberts*

**Open year round** • Western and Mexican saddles • Quarter horses, Mexican ponies • All skill levels • 2 and 3 day pack trips – camping • Unlimited riding • Ranch stays • Guest capacity 6 • Horseshoes • Badminton • Volleyball • Children welcome.

Rancho Madrono is 83 acres of pine-oak forest overlooking scenic Lake Patzcuaro in the volcanic belt of Southwestern Mexico. Unlimited unpaved roads and trails meander up the mountainside and through quaint villages, with breathtaking views of the lake and mountains. Highland towns are rich in Spanish architecture and Indian flavor. Local crafts and festivals draw visitors from around the world. Sightseeing trips offered. Options include day rides and one or two night pack trips. You'll see rural Mexico in a unique way, meet its friendly people, experience its culture and taste its cuisine. Accommodations are charming and meals delicious. Activities are available for non-riders. American owned and operated.

**Country House / Point To Point / Camping**

## THE ANDES HIGH MOUNTAIN ADVENTURE

Intiexpress Otavalo - Adventure Tours - Horseback Riding
Sucre 11-10 entre Morales y Colon, Otavalo, Ecuador
Tel: (593)-6-921-436 Fax: (593)-6-920-737
*Contact: Nuria de Vaca*

**Open all year** • Spanish saddles • 45 Criollo horses (Mustang like) • All skill levels • Cross country Andean Mountain rides • Customized riding packages, two day rides (stay in small village), day rides to Otacachi Volcano with lake inside • Children welcome • Stays in 300 year old Hacienda • Maximum 10 riders per group • 60 miles from Quito • Transfers arranged

Welcome (Bienvenida) to the breath taking beauty of the High Andes of Ecuador, a place of remarkable beauty and a rich and lasting culture dating back to Ecuador's original Indian inhabitants. It is like moving back in history to a peaceful world, as yet undisturbed by the modernization that is sweeping our nations' larger cities. Our horses are well trained, native Criollos and our qualified guides can arrange a horse suitable for your level of skill. Our prices are extremely reasonable. Riders stay at a charming 300 year old Hacienda. All types of riding and non riding adventures can be arranged to suit your individual needs.

# EUROPE

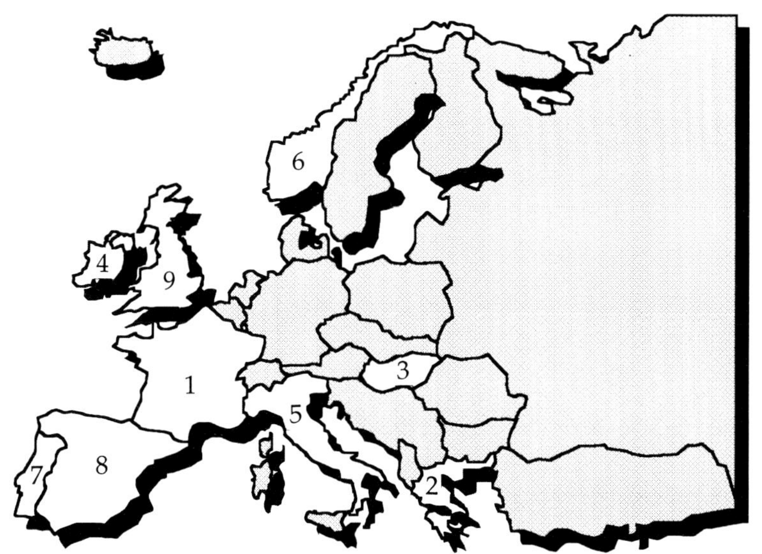


1 – France
2 – Greece
3 – Hungary
4 – Ireland
5 – Italy
6 – Norway
7 – Portugal
8 – Spain
9 – United Kingdom

PHOTO: HORSE CLASSICS CALENDAR

**Point to Point / Inn to Inn / Cottages**

## FERME EQUESTRE DE LA FOLIE PANIER

F 78980 Breval – Ile de France
Tel/Fax: (33)-134-78-33-88
*Contact: Regis Chomel de Jarnieu*

**Open all year** • English tack, Canadian saddles for ponies • 10 French saddlebreds, 9 ponies • Trail riding from farm • 1 to 6 day inn to inn rides • 2 room cottage on site, several in village • Special children's camp for parents who wish to enjoy inn to inn • English speaking counselors • All skill levels for based trail riding • Intermediate skill level for inn to inn rides • Outdoor tennis, nearby golf • March 21 to Nov. 11 • French, English, German and Spanish spoken • 60 km from Paris

We are a 75 acre, century old livestock farm with several 2 room cottages on the property. We can provide enjoyable riding vacations for adults who stay at our farm while providing a full range of counselor supported programs for children and teens. Reliable baby-sitters are also available. There are many local historical sights that you can visit on horseback. Tennis and golf are available in season. Enjoy our 2 to 6 day inn to inn rides. Riders will encounter gently rolling green hills with opportunities for long gallops while passing old stone houses and small villages. Twice monthly, our treks take us to 12th and 15th century chateau-hotels, a very romantic setting. Our multi-lingual guide Regis leads all the treks.

**Farmhouse**

## LE HARAS DE LA PERFIDE ALBION

Le Bois Foucher, St Maurice Les Charency
61190 Tourouvre, France
Tel: (33)-33-25-63-61 Fax: (33)-33-25-63-95
after Sept: Tel: (33)-02-33-25-63-61 Fax: (33)-02-33-25-63-95
*Contact: Graham Wenman*

**Open all year** • English and Western saddle • 30 horses • Spanish, Akhal Teke, British Native • All skill levels • Hacking • Fishing • Facility for clients' horses • Nearby golf, tennis, swimming

The Haras de la Perfide Albion is a small, family run stud farm in Normandy. There are many local attractions, including the French National Stud. PARIS, VERSAILLES and CHARTRES are within easy reach. Accommodation is in centrally heated, en-suite rooms in our farmhouse, B & B or self catering. There is a good selection of local restaurants or we can provide dinner, including vegetarian. Our main activity is hacking; there are more than 1000 miles of tracks (off road) including State forests. You can enjoy a 2 day trail ride as part of your holiday. Visit the local cider maker and a local chateau.

**Point to Point / Hotel to Hotel**

## PROVENCE-TRAIL

Le Haras de la Manueye, Route de la Campane
13770 Venelles, France
Tel/Fax: (33)-42-54-1326
*Contact: Jean Claude Chouard*

**Open March through Nov.** • English tack – "Forestier" saddles • 6 riders + guide • For proficient riders • Average saddle time 6 to 7 hours • 6 day trips • Shorter 2, 3 day trips • Spanish and Barb horses • Hotel to hotel • English (... No Perfect ..!) and Italian spoken

Provence is the land of cicadas and olive trees, of fields of lavender and ancient hill-top villages. Here, the scene is lit by the strong southern sun, the atmosphere unmistakably Mediterranean. Ride fine Spanish horses through this magical evocative region which for many is the most beautiful of France. The guided ride from hotel to hotel is top of the range for horses, guiding, hotels and equipment The ride is exciting for proficient riders. We offer superb Spanish horses and English tack, high-quality accommodations, luggage transportation and a warm, sunny climate.

**Bed & Breakfast**

## FERME DE LAUNAY

37210 Chancay, Indre Et Loire, France
Tel/Fax: (33)-47-522-821
after Oct 1996: (33)-02-47-522-821
*Contact: M et Mme J.P. Schweizer*

**Open all year** • English Tack • Thoroughbreds • 5 horses (4 riders) • Guest capacity of 6 • Adults only • Intermediate ability required • 2 to 3 hours riding per day • Nearby golf, tennis and swimming • Fishing on property

Eighteenth century farmhouse lovingly restored. Luxurious, comfortable, ensuite bedrooms. Gourmet meals served "en famille." Special inclusive package (room, breakfast, dinner and riding) Oct. through May. Vouvray vineyards and villages, forests past private chateaux. Wine-tastings, visits to Cadre Noir at Saumur, Haras National (French national stud-stallions of many breeds at Blois). See chateaux of the Loire, Tours, Amboise on your own. 150 miles from Paris, 2 hours by car, 50 minutes by TGV train. A NON-SMOKING HOUSE. Fluent English, German and some Italian spoken.

**Point to Point / Stationary**

## HIPPOCAMPUS FARM

Katigiorgi 37006 Argalasti, Greece
Tel: (30)-423-71076 Fax: (30)-423-71072
*Contact: Eric Lefort*

**Open March 15 to Nov. 15** • Point to point dates mid April to mid Oct. • English tack and McClellan saddles • 15 Horses • Greek horses – Arab-Barb type horses • Inn to Inn – 6 to 9 day rides • Camping rides 6 days + 13 day Olympus to Pilion ride in July • Average saddle time 5 hours • Competent and fit riders for point to point • Stationary vacations – all skill levels • Inland trails – beach riding • Delicious Greek foods • Seafood specialties • English, Greek, French, German and Czech spoken

Hippocampus farm is on a hill above the sea at the tip of the peninsula of Pilion, known in antiquity as the mountain of Centaurs, the mythical creatures that were half horse and half man, who shared with the nymphs the dwellings of deep lush forest, alternating with olive and fruit orchards, surrounded everywhere by the crystal clear Aegean sea. You may enjoy a charming relaxed riding vacation at the farm, breakfast at the farm and other meals at the harbor's tavern. Our inn to inn style rides require riders who can deal with a long day of riding involving all 3 gaits. We stay at quality guest houses (converted from mansions) and comfortable hotels. Luggage is transferred for you by vehicle on all point to point rides.

**Point to point / Inn to Inn**

## HORTOBAGY TOUR

Hortobagy, Hungary

*Contact: Anna Petterson*
Ibusz International, American Travel Abroad
250 W. 57th St., NYC, NY 10107 USA
Tel: 212-586-5230 Tel: 1-800-367-7878 Fax: 212-581-7925

**Open April 1 through Oct. 31** • English tack • Average time in saddle 3-1/2 to 5 hours • 9 day, 8 night program with 6 days of riding • Airport transfers from Budapest • Guide and escort coach • Special wine tastings • Experienced riders only • Full service

Our riding tours are recommended for experienced riders only. Trails are designed to go across open lands, woods and fields, wherever possible. Daily rides are about 20 to 30 miles. Trips begin with Saturday arrival at Budapest and a transfer by escorted coach to Hubertus Inn in Poroszlo for a dinner with wine. Sunday is a full day ride, with picnic lunch, as is Monday and Tuesday. On Tuesday, luggage is transferred to Epona Hotel in Hortobagy. Wednesday is a day of leisure, Thursday and Friday are full day rides. Saturday is a half day ride, lunch, a transfer to a Budapest hotel and a farewell dinner followed by breakfast on Sunday.

**Point to Point / Inn to Inn**

## EL RANCHO HORSE HOLIDAYS LTD.

Ballyard, Tralee, Co. Kerry
Tel: (353)-66-21840 Fax: (353)-66-21840
*Contact: William J. O'Connor*

**Open May through Sept. 10** • English tack • 16 horses • Irish Hunters, Connemara Ponies • 10 rider limit • 3 and 6 day vacations • Stationary and point to point • 4 to 5 hours riding each day • Intermediate and advanced skill levels • Nearby golf, tennis, shooting, fishing, swimming (indoor/outdoor), sauna.

*DINGLE PENINSULA TRAIL RIDES*

Get away from it all. Enjoy real freedom. Feel at one with nature as you experience the adventure and magic of the fascinating Dingle Peninsula Trails. Ride through our rugged mountains and quiet little tracks which are lined with fuchsia hedges and gallop on golden beaches with the ever -breaking surf. Your luggage is transported by car. Established in 1967, El Rancho is approved by the Association of Riding Establishments, Irish Horse Board and Board Failte. Located 1 mile from Tralee. Brochure and video available on request, by quoting ref. no. W.R.V.' 96.

**Point to Point / Inn to Inn**

## CLEW BAY TRAIL & DRUMMINDOO STUD AND EQUITATION CENTRE

Westport, Co Mayo, Ireland
Tel: (353)-98-25616 Fax: (353)-98-26709
*Contact: Paraic Foy ICES*

**Open all year** • English tack • 8 Connemaras, 8 Irish hunters • Residential training center • Indoor and outdoor • Basic instruction • Hacking • 3 day Clew Bay Ride • 4 to 5 hours riding daily • All skill levels welcome • Bord Failte approved farmhouse accommodations • Golf, sailing, fishing nearby

The Clew Bay Trail operates from mid-May through Oct. and takes the rider to a different location each day for 4 to 5 hours of fantastic riding from Murrinsk under Croagh Patrick to Louisburgh to Killadoon. The ride occurs along the exciting Atlantic coast line and much of the ride is on the beach! Accommodations are provided in farmhouses along the route. The equestrian centre provides instruction from beginners to competition level. Nearby Westport, a handsome planned town, includes a championship golf course, a sailing centre, fishing and shooting.

**Guest House**

## BALLYCORMAC HOUSE

Aglish, Near Borrisokane, Co. Tipperary, Ireland
Tel: (353)-67-21129 Fax: (353)-67-21200
*Contact: Herb / Christine Quigley*

**Open all year** • English tack • 40 horses • Irish Hunters, Connemaras, Colored Ponies • Indoor riding • Cross country • Fox hunting • Lessons • Nearby – golf, shooting, fishing • Guest capacity 9 to 12 • 5 ensuite rooms

From March through October, we arrange riding programs including trail riding, hacking, a based 7 day trail ride through the Slieve Aughty Mountains and along the River Shannon, challenging cross country courses, show jumping and lessons. Custom riding programs can be designed using three unique equestrian centers: Shannon Trekking, Flowerhill Equestrian Farm and Milchem Equestrian Centre. From October to March our specialty is fox hunting. We are ideally situated near a dozen different hunts. Hirelings are always local and matched to each rider's skill. The atmosphere at our 300 year old home is of a private country home with warm cozy en-suite accommodations, award winning food and attention to detail.

# Horseback Riding through the Enchanted Landscapes of Italy

Horseback riding in Italy is truly a unique experience for riders of all levels. There is no better way of getting a real feel for Italian culture and lifestyle than spending time in the countryside where ancient traditions and folklore remain intact. It is an Italy that only a handful of privileged tourists are able to discover.

The rides offered here are based in two of the country's most spectacularly beautiful and historically rich regions: TUSCANY AND UMBRIA. The terrain varies greatly within short distances from steep mountain ranges to soft hills lined with vineyards and dotted with olive groves to open fields of bright yellow sunflowers. These colorful landscapes are interrupted at various points by medieval hilltop villages or the stately castles and villas of the Chianti area.

Accommodations in original 100-year old stone farmhouses add to the authentic ambiance, topped off with superb homemade meals made from fresh local produce. Visits to nearby farms offer the possibility of observing first hand the production of cheeses, salami, wine and olive oil depending on the season.

Make a trip to Italy and all that is memorable by combining it with your love of riding!

*Arriverderci!*

**Inn / Inn to Inn**

## ANTICO CASALE DI SCANSANO

Loc. Castagneta, Scansano (GR) 58054, Italy
Tel: (39)-564- 507219 Fax: (39)-564-507-805
*Contact: United States Representative*

## HIDDEN TREASURES OF ITALY

934 Elmwood Ave., Wilmette, Illinois 60091
Tel: 847-853-1312 Fax: 847-853-1340
E mail: htreasure@aol.com

**Open March to January** • English tack • 18 horses • Argentian stock, Arabian Crossbreeds • Intermediate skill level • Daily trail riding • "Maremma 7 Day Exploration Ride " • Combined sailing and riding tours • Swimming • Mountain bikes • Sauna • Archery • Adults only • Some English spoken • 150 km. north of Rome airport (Leonardo da Vinci)

The Antico Casale is a hundred year old farmhouse, completely restored to a four star property while conserving its original architectural features. It is located in the southern part of Tuscany called "Maremma," or the wild West of Italy for its tradition of cattle farms. All amenities are offered within very comfortable rooms decorated with country antiques. Typical Tuscan dishes are served in the adjoining restaurant, including home made pastas and wine from our own vineyards. For horse lovers, the rides in this spectacular and unspoiled countryside are unmatched. Daily outings include visits to medieval villages, Etruscan ruins and neighboring farms.

**Inn / Residential Riding Center**

## IL PARETAIO

San Filippo 50021 Barberino val d'Elsa (FI), Italy
Tel: (39)-55-80-59-218 Fax: (39)-55-80-59-231
*Contact: Christina De Marchi in Italy or*

**United States Representative**

## HIDDEN TREASURES OF ITALY

934 Elmwood Avenue, Wilmette, Illinois, 60091, US
Tel: 847-853-1312 Fax: 847-853-1340
E mail: htreasure@aol.com

**Open all year** • English tack • 25 horses • Thoroughbreds, Arabian, Italian saddlebred, Lusitanos • All skill levels • Trail riding • Dressage lessons beginner to advanced • Swimming • Tennis • Special children's program • Guest capacity 18 • French and English spoken • Nearest airports – Florence (Firenze) 50 km north., Rome 300 km south

Il Paretaio is a highly acclaimed riding center in the hills midway between Florence and Sienna – a perfect location for exploring Tuscany. Its owners have 30 years of equestrian experience and maintain a stable of 25 well trained horses. Courses from beginner to advanced dressage are offered. Guests may take picturesque rides on horseback past medieval churches and ancient farmhouses and enjoy nice picnics. Six rooms, each with a private bathroom, are located within the renovated stone house which was built in the 1700s. Each is decorated with dried flowers, lace curtains, antiques and equestrian prints. Meals feature traditional Tuscan cuisine and local wine and are served at an enormous table in front of the hearth.

***Directions:*** From highway exit Florence Certosa – Go towards Siena – Exit Tavernelle – After Barberino val d'Elsa, right S. Felippo

**Inn to Inn**

## AZIENDA MALVARINA

Via Malvarina 32, Assisi (PG), 06080 Italy
Tel/Fax: (39)-75-806-4280
*Contact: United States Representative*

## HIDDEN TREASURES OF ITALY

934 Elmwood Ave., Wilmette, Illinois 50091, USA
Tel: 847-853-1312 Fax: 847-853-1340
E mail: htreasure@aol.com

**Open all year** • English and Western tack • 8 horses • Italian saddle-bred, Argentine breed • Intermediate skill level • 3, 4 and 5 day riding packages • Riding lessons available • Medical insurance required • Nearest airport – Rome 200 km.

At just a few miles away from medieval Assisi, in the heart of Umbria, is the Malvarina farm. Guests are housed within several small stone cottages, individually decorated with typical country antiques. Horses have always played a vital role in the lives of the people of this area. The Fabrizi family has brought back this tradition by organizing horseback riding treks through the nearby Subasio Mountains. This unique combination of enchanted landscapes dotted with richly historical towns creates a fascinating riding experience. Guests gather at the end of the day in the cozy rustic dining room where Mamma Maria shows off her culinary talents using ancient regional recipes.

**Residential Riding Center**

## LA CASELLA

Strada La Casella 4, Ficulle (TR), 05016 Italy
Tel: (39)-763-86684 Tel: (39)-763-86075 Fax: (39)-763-86684
*Contact: United States Representative*

## HIDDEN TREASURES OF ITALY

934 Elmwood Ave., Wilmette, Illinois 60091, USA
Tel: 847-853-1312 Fax: 847-853-1340
E mail: htreasure@aol.com

**Open March to January** • English tack • 40 horses • Different breeds • All skill levels • Lessons (riding, jumping, dressage) • Cross-country • Trail rides • Fox hunting • Special summer night rides with candle-light dinner • Swimming • Fishing • Archery • Mountain Bike • Pool • Bar • Conference room • English, German, French, Spanish, Swedish spoken • Nearest airport Rome – 120 km

La Casella farm, immersed in an ocean of green landscapes, was once upon a time inhabited by humble farmers. The four houses of the estate have been restored to provide every possible comfort and to guarantee absolute relaxation in the peace and quiet of the Umbrian countryside. In a warm, cozy atmosphere, we offer the tastes of local "down-home" cooking long associated with the traditions of the area. Signora Maria's cooking is richly restorative and we always make it a point to serve dishes that are in tune with the cycles of the seasons. We offer a large, nationally acclaimed riding center with a complete and modernized structure: jumping-field, dressage, a ring and a cross-country field. Also organized are delightful day-long rides through the unspoiled countryside. Halfway between Rome and Florence, on the A1 motorway exit "Fabro." Follow directions "PARRANO" for 7 km, then follow signs for "LA CASELLA" for another 6 KM.

**Point to Point**

## FJELLRITTET

N-2950 Skammestein, Norway
Tel: (47)-61-34-1101 Fax: (47)-61-34-1524
*Contact: Bente Okshovd / Torgeir Svalesen*

**Open June 30 to Aug. 17 for week trips** • Open until Sept. 9 for weekends and special group arrangements • English style • 30 horses • Norwegian cold bloods, Island horses, Welsh and Connemara ponies • 7 day, 6 night trips • Weekend trips • Experienced riders • Minimum age 15 years, 12 if accompanied by parents • Guest capacity of 22 • Rafting • Hiking • Local handicrafts • Boat excursions • English and German spoken

Our Sunday to Saturday trek offers experienced riders an opportunity to walk, trot, canter and gallop on our well conditioned horses through the beautiful mountain region of Jotunheimen. The rides are supported by automobiles which move your luggage to the 3 hotels and 2 mountain huts we use on the trip. The terrain varies from spectacularly beautiful rugged mountain passes to sandy beaches perfect for a gallop. We like to share our knowledge of horses and the area with you through a series of slides and discussions. On Wednesday, we break up our 20 to 40 kilometer a day pace by offering rafting, boat excursions, hiking and local handicraft or rest and relaxation. Please call, fax or write for details.

**Hotel / Residential Riding Centre**

## HOTEL RURAL A COUTADA / CENTRO HIPICO A COUTADA

Quintas das tripas, Altouguia da Baleia, 2520 Peniche
Tel: (351)-62 759-733 Tel: (351)-62-750-2520 Fax: (351)-62-759-733
*Contact: Victor Jorge*

**Open all year** • English (Portuguese) saddles • 40 horses • Lusitano horses • Lessons • Cross-country • Trail riding • 4 and 5 day riding tours • Up to 3 hours riding each day • Intermediate and advanced riders • 33 ensuite rooms • Pool • Tennis • Miniature golf • English, French and German spoken • Nearest airport – Lisbon

Situated in the center of the Western Tourism Region, 75 km from Lisbon and 2 km from the sea. A mild winter and a warm summer make us a perfect year round property. Each room is fully equipped with AC, satellite TV and full size bathroom. Our pool and comfortable bar invite relaxation. We offer transportation to and from the airport, sightseeing tours and car rental facilities. Our four star riding center is perfect for beginning riders as well as the experienced horsemen. We also offer relaxed 3 and 4 day riding tours through the countryside for experienced riders. Please call or write for our multilingual color brochures.

**Point to Point / Inn to Inn**

## CABALGAR RUTAS ALTERNATIVAS

18412-Bubion, Granada, Spain
Tel/Fax: (34)-58-76-3135
*Contact: Rafael Belmonte*

**Open all year** • English, Western and Spanish tack • 15 horses • Arabian-Spanish crossbred • 4 to 6 hours a day riding • Intermediate skill level required • 1 to 9 day treks • Beach swimming in season • Jacuzzi • Massage • Granda, Malaga nearest airports • Spanish, French, English and a little German spoken • Member: WORLDWIDE ORGANIZATION OF EQUESTRIAN TOURISM

*THE SECRET ANDALUSIA – SIERRA NEVADA ON HORSEBACK*

Discover the beautiful mountains of Las Alpujarras, the desert of Tabernas and the beaches of Almeria. Enjoy an authentic Spanish atmosphere ably hosted by Rafael Belmonte (fluent English, 14 yrs. experience). Imagine trekking through centuries old horseshoe paths that snake through ravines alongside streams fed by melting snows. The striking geography and incredible altitude changes produce an incredible array of flora and fauna that allows trekkers from all over the world to have a memorable and surprising experience. Treks from 1 to 9 days. Accommodations are always in the area's best hotels. Rooms are with private bathrooms. Excellent local cuisine.

**Inn**

## FINCA LA MOTA

Alhaurin el Grande, WWRV
Malaga, Espana 29120
Tel: (34)-5-249-0901 Tel/Fax: (34)-5-259-4120
*Contact: Arun or Jean*

**Open all year** • English style tack – Spanish saddles • 4 Spanish Crossbreds • 1, 2 and 3 hour rides • All skill levels • As many hours as you desire • Tennis • Swimming • Miniature golf • Children's playground • Nearby golf course • Nearby Mediterranean beaches • Restaurant • Guest capacity of 26 • English, French, German spoken

Finca La Mota is a farmhouse, but more so a home, providing a relaxing family holiday which is informal and unpretentious. We offer a swimming pool, tennis court, miniature golf and for the horse riders in your family, peaceful rides through stunning scenery. We are not an organized riding holiday. You can ride whenever and for how long you choose. We are an ideal base for visiting Granada, Ronda and Sevilla. We are only 15 minutes from the Mediterranean beaches, 1 kilometer from a golf course. Children are very welcome. Our restaurant features an outdoor barbecue and Indian specialties. We have a children's menu and vegetarian meals.

**Inn to Inn / Hotel**

## HURRICANE HOTEL

Tarifa, Andalusia, Spain
Tel: 34-56-684-919 Fax: 34-56-680-329
*Contact: James or Andrea*

**Open all year** • English or Western tack • 12 horses • Hispano-Arab • Riding at hotel • 7 day treks through Andalusia from Tarifa to Ronda • 6 hours a day in saddle on treks • Intermediate and advanced riders • Farmhouses and inns • Hotel based riding, all skill levels • Beach riding • Windsurfing • Health club • Masseur • Mountain bikes • Swimming pools • Fine foods • 28 rooms • 2 Luxury suites • Guest capacity at hotel 72 • English, French, German spoken • Nearest airport Malaga or Seville

Riders may organize their holiday around a stay at the beautiful Hurricane Hotel and enjoy spectacular beach riding in Tarifa, a fishing village located on the most southerly tip of Europe with spectacular views of Africa across the straits of Gibraltar. Hurricane Hotel also organizes exclusive treks for small groups of friends to the historic Arab built city of Ronda, perched in the sierra high above Marbella. We ride from the beach, north through cork forests and mountain scenery, avoiding all roads. We stay in small hotels or farmhouses. Minimum four friends or family group with good riding ability. Phone for further information and to fix dates and prices.

**Point to Point / Inn to Inn Type**

## RUTAS A CABALLO TURISMO ECUESTRE ARTZINIEGA

Barrio Campo de Futbol, 6, Artziniega 01474, Alava, Spain
Tel/Fax: (34)-45-396-060
*Contact: Carmello Gutierrez Vallejo*

**Open all year** • English style tack • 18 horses • Anglo Hispano Arabians • Average saddle time 4 to 6 hours a day • Experienced riders only • 2 day stationary riding holidays • 7 day full service treks • Special 5 day rides in June, Aug. and Sept. • Limit 10 to a ride • Guided by trained, knowledgeable guides • Near Bilbao – transfers to property • English, French and German spoken • Member: WORLDWIDE ORGANIZATION OF EQUESTRIAN TOURISM

Riding through Basque country in Northern Spain. Discover the most western part of Basque country on our responsive, well conditioned horses riding between the mountains and green valleys covered with historical monuments. All rides include meals and accommodations at charming rural hotels or rustic farmhouses. You will enjoy the delicious cuisine typical of the area. Our riding program includes a stationary two night stay in a country hotel, a weekly inn to inn type ride and a 5 day, 4 night ride "By the Iron Road." This is an unforgettable riding experience as you travel through the ancient historical city of Bizkaia. Dates of this trip are June 22–26, Aug. 3–7, Aug. 17–21 and Sept. 2–6.

**Point to point / Monastery to Monastery**

## ESCOLA D'EQUITACIO SON MENUT

3 Volta, 3040 (Cami de Son Negre)
07208, Felanitx (Mallorca) Spain
Tel: (34)-71-582920 Fax: (34)-71-582920
*Contact: Reservations*

**Open Sept. to May for Monastery ride** • Open all year for local riding • English tack – Spanish saddles • 11 horses • Trotana • Average saddle time each day 3 hours to 7 hours • All skill levels • Ride capacity is 8 riders • 6 day 5 night ride • Airport or hotel transfers • English, German, French spoken • Member: WORLD-WIDE ORGANIZATION OF EQUESTRIAN TOURISM.

Although Majorca is know for its beaches and tourist centres, there is another Majorca of countryside, cultural and ecological conditions that make possible an adventure in contact with the island's nature and history. Our ride covers 166 kilometers in 6 days, with nightly stays at the island's ancient monasteries dating back as far as the fourteenth century. You will enjoy the typical food of the island served in locations that offer fantastic views! Our trips are supported by vehicle and experienced guides. Our horses are Trotana. Call or write for more information.

**Point to Point / Stationary**

## HIPICA DELTA

Paseo Riomar s/n
Deltebre, Tarragona, Spain
Tel: (34)-3588-23-01 Fax: (34)-3588-25-86 Mobile tel: (34)-085-999-71
*Contact: Dolores Elias*

**Open Sept. to June for riding holidays** • Open all year • English and Western tack • 20 horses • Crossbreds • 1 to 5 day rides • Farmhouse to farmhouse – other options possible • 6 hours a day riding • All skill levels • 175 km from Barcelona, 75 km from Tarragona • French and English spoken • Transfers possible from airports • Member: WORLDWIDE ORGANIZATION OF EQUESTRIAN TOURISM

Hipico Delta is a 5 minute ride from Mediterranean beaches. We offer 1 day to 5 day rides. Our rides move us through the geography, history and culture of the Ebro Delta. Trail riders move along beaches and rivers, through rice fields and marshes, to the famous Marquesa lighthouse, through dunes and olive groves, and along Encanyissada Lake where the ducks abound. We offer trips from 1 day to 1 week. The weather is moderate, even in our winter season. Accommodations and meals on point to point rides are selected with the goal of giving riders a feel for the daily life of the region, with all its variety and richness. Holidays may be customized to suit small groups or families.

**Point to Point / Inn to Inn / Stationary**

## EXMOOR RIDING HOLIDAYS

North Wheddon Farm
Wheddon Cross, Minehead, Somerset TA24 7EX, England
Tel: (44)-1643 841224 Tel/Fax: (44)-1643 841159
*Contact: Jon Trouton*

**Open April to Nov.** • English tack • 18 horses • Thoroughbreds, Hunters, Cobs • 14.3hh to 17 hh. • Weight limit 230 pounds • Advanced riding skills • 5 and 6 day trips • Ride capacity 9 • Also stationary based holidays • Residential riding centre • Approved by British Horse Society • Member: Assoc. of British Riding Schools

Enjoying the mild climate of South West England. Exmoor is wild, beautiful and magnificent riding country. Exciting riding on very good and exceptionally fit horses for small groups of competent adults riding as friends, not one behind the other. Stay near the centre of the National Park in our comfortable old listed house, in the village inn and ride out daily or tour with different overnight stops. Guests may help look after the horse. Good food. Log fires. Attractive garden. 25th season. Approved by Tourist Board.

**Residential Riding Centre**

## HAYFIELD RIDING CENTRE

Hazlehead Park, Aberdeen AB1 8BB, Scotland
Tel: (44)-1224-315703 Fax: (44)-1224-313834
Web: http://www.scotweb.com/equinet/ (changes in Jan.)
E mail: equinet@wintermute.co.uk (changes in Jan.)
*Contact: John / Sue Crawford*

**Open all year** • English or Western saddles • 45 horses and ponies • Well trained and happy • All skill levels • Riding hours to suit • Instruction • Daily trail rides through forest, moorland, mountains or beaches • Two indoor schools • Large outdoor jumping arena • Cross country course • Dressage arenas • Many competitions • Pony club base • Polo practice field • Accommodation on site for 10 • Non riders welcome • Surrounded by golf courses • 5 minutes from Aberdeen • Theatres, restaurants, nightlife and shopping • 15 minutes from international airport • Instructor training centre • Fully approved • We also teach clinics worldwide •

Come to Hayfield in " Bonnie Scotland" and enjoy just as much riding challenge, fun and pleasure as you can handle! You can either challenge yourself, learning new skills in dressage, jumping, side saddle, western, polo or eventing and cross-country jumping or just choose to lay back in the saddle for hours and soak in the beauty of Scotland with it's Lochs, lofty mountains, forests, beaches, and historic coastline with it's castles and whiskey distilleries. You decide, we provide and work out a programme just for you, your family or your group. Whatever your choice, we can assure you of good instruction and hours of good fun in the saddle on happy, well trained horses or ponies, while being surrounded by the very best of Scotland.

*See Color Photo Page 113*

**Point to Point**

## HIGHLAND ICELANDIC HORSE TREKKING

Ardechive, Achnacarry, Inverness-Shire, Scotland PH34-4EL
Tel: (44)-1397-712-427
http: //www.compulink.co.uk/~jnelson/highland.htm
*Contact: Andrew Carson*

**Open March to Oct.** • English tack • Icelandic Horses, Highland Ponies (10) • Capacity – 6 riders • 3, 4, 5 and 6 day trips • Average ride time 6 to 7 hours • Intermediate and advanced riders • Fishing • Member: Trekking & Riding Society Scotland, Affiliated with British Horse Society

Trekking and trail-ride holidays on Icelandic Horses through spectacular highland mountains and glens are available. Tours are from 3 to 7 days on these sturdy, nimble trekking horses with experienced and qualified local guides. Pack ponies and vehicle backup. Accommodation in B&B, bothies and camping. Use of ancient routes in an area steeped in Scottish Clan history. Situated on the shores of Loch Arkaig in the heart of the West Highlands. 1 hr., 2 hr. and day rides from our centre. Local traditional accommodation arranged for residential riding. Discover the beautiful scenery in a unique fashion.

**Farmhouse / Inn to Inn style**

## CAE LAGO

Ffarmers, Llanwrda, Dyfed, SA19 8LZ, Wales, United Kingdom
Tel: (44)-1558-650303
*Contact: Reservations*

**Open mid-March to end of Nov for extended riding programs**
• Open all year • English tack • 20 horses • Trail horses, Welsh Cobs • All skill levels • 2 to 5 day mid week breaks • 2 and 3 day trail rides – stopovers in country pubs and/or youth hostel • Full weeks • 4 to 5 hours riding each day • Weight limit 210 pounds • Guest capacity 12 • Minimum age 17 years • Approved by Brit. Horse Society, Wales Tourist Board Accredited Activity Centre • A few hours from international airports

Over the last 30 years, Cae lago has established itself as one of the most popular riding holiday centres in Wales. Its location on the edge of the magnificent Cambrian Mountains ensures some of the most spectacular riding country and varied wildlife in Britain. Roman roads and ancient drovers tracks take you past clear mountain streams as they tumble down into shady valleys. You'll find everything about your stay at Cae lago informal and relaxed. Our Victorian farm house is clean and comfortable. Plentiful quantities of home cooked food and the occasional stroll down to the local pubs will ensure that you'll recover fully from each day's exertions.

**Farmhouse / Point to Point by Application**

## GRANGE TREKKING CENTRE

Capel-Y-Ffin, Agbergravenny, Gwent,
NP77NP United Kingdom
Tel: (44)-1873-890-215
*Contact: Jessica Griffiths*

**Open March through Nov.** • English tack • 45 horses • Welsh cobs, Shire Arabs and Thoroughbred crosses • Weekly treks (return to farm), weekend treks, Inn to Inn style by application, day and half day rides • All skill levels • Handicapped riders welcome • Children 6 and older may ride • Farm guest house accommodations • Full service riding packages • Nearby fishing, golf, canoeing and more • Airport transfers arranged • Member: Wales Trekking & Riding Assoc.

We offer weekly riding holidays with wonderful views, lush green valleys, waterfalls, wildlife and heather covered mountain tops where you can see for miles. Our area offers many chances to trot and canter for those wishing to do so. Instruction and demonstrations on grooming and tacking up are given. All ages and abilities are cared for by our experienced guides on quality horses with high standards of safety and with the privilege of panoramic breathtaking views. We welcome you to join us in our award winning old Victorian farm guest house with its friendly atmosphere, where, after an exhilarating day in the saddle, we will serve hearty traditional food and provide comfortable accommodations.

# North America

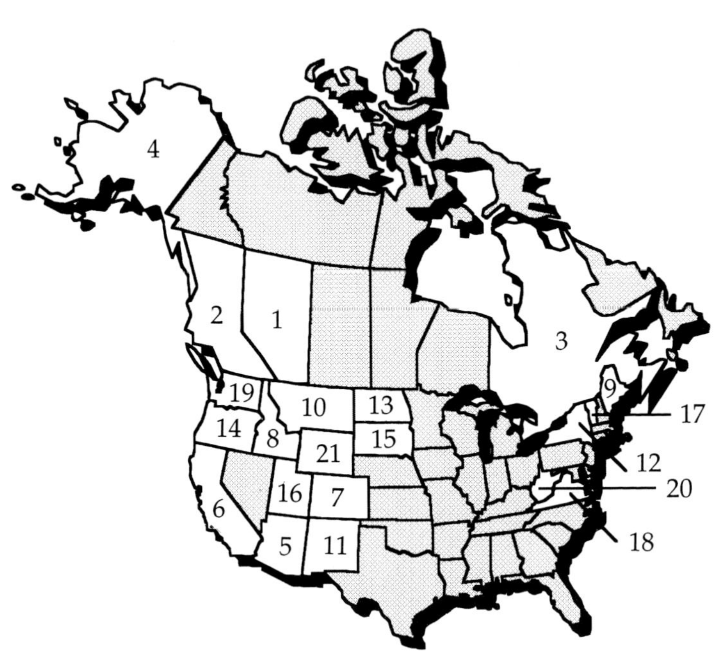


1 – Alberta
2 – British Columbia
3 – Quebec
4 – Alaska
5 – Arizona
6 – California
7 – Colorado
8 – Idaho
9 – Maine
10 – Montana
11 – New Mexico
12 – New York
13 – North Dakota
14 – Oregon
15 – South Dakota
16 – Utah
17 – Vermont
18 – Virginia
19 – Washington
20 – West Virginia
21 – Wyoming

**Guest Ranch / Dude**

## BLACK CAT GUEST RANCH

PO Box 626, Hinton, Alberta T7V 1X6
Tel: 403-865-3084 Tel: 800-859-6840 Fax: 403-865-1924
*Contact: Amber Hayward*

**Open all year** • Western tack • 25 horses • Quarter horses • Riding mid May to mid Oct. • Minimum riding age 8 • Guest Capacity 40 • Hiking • Rafting – July, Aug. • Cross-country skiing • Murder mystery weekends • Writing, photography and art workshops • Gym equipment • Hot tub • Member: Alberta Guest Ranch Assoc.

The Black Cat Guest Ranch is a small, friendly wilderness resort with beautiful trails for riding or hiking. Each of the 16 rooms has a knock-out view of the front range of the Canadian Rockies plus full private bathrooms. Queen size beds and non-smoking rooms are available. Savor our delicious home-style meals in the company of fellow guests from around the globe. Summer features: Cadomin cave expeditions, watercolor workshop, weekly line dance evenings, raft excursions and frequent barbecues. Just one hour's drive from Jasper – you can enjoy day trips to take in the attractions before returning to your secluded hide-away.

**Outfitter**

## ALBERTA FRONTIER GUIDING & OUTFITTING

PO Box 1868, Sundre, Alberta T0M 1X0
Tel: 403-638-2897 Fax: 403-638-2594
E Mail: frontier @cadusion.com
*Contact: Judy Walker*

**Open year round** • Western tack • 8 to 12 riders • 3, 5 and 7 day pack trips through Rockies • 5 hours average time in saddle • Also up to 10 day base camp • Daily riding or combination whitewater rafting • Riding • Winter sleigh rides • Photography trips • Member: Alberta Outfitters Assoc.

**Outfitter**

## HORSEBACK ADVENTURE, LTD.

Box 73, Brule, Alberta T0E-0C0
Tel: 403-865-4777 Fax: 403-875-5433
*Contact: Tom or Shawn Vinson*

**Open June 1 – Sept. 15** • Western tack • 60 horses • Percheron, Quarter horses • Children welcome • All skill levels • 15 people to each adventure • 6 to 14 days • Moving tent camps • 4 to 6 hours riding each day • Cow camps May 15 to Oct. 15 • 3 to 5 hours riding each day • 5 Day trips • Lodge • Cabin accommodations • Member: Alberta Outfitters Assoc.

**Outfitter**

## HOLIDAY ON HORSEBACK

PO Box 2280, Banff, Alberta T0L0C0
Tel: 403-762-4551 Fax: 403-762-8130
*Contact: Ron Warner*

**Open May through Oct.** • Western tack • 300 horses • Quarter horses • Trail rides • Day rides • Carriage tours • Breakfast and Evening Steakfrys • Covered Wagon Luncheon ride • 2, 3, 4, 5 and 6 day tenting pack trips • Based trips from one wilderness lodge to another • Average saddle time 4 hours • Aug. 30 to Sept. 30 Adults only • Member: Alberta Outfitters Association

For the last 34 years, Warner Guiding & Outfitting has been upholding the back country tradition of horseback riding through the Canadian Rockies in Banff National Park. Easily accessible by car or bus, Banff is only a 1-1/2 hour drive from the Calgary International Airport. Right now, the exchange rate saves you 34 cents on the US dollar, which is a great advantage for you! Join us for a holiday from 2 to 6 days on a tenting pack trip or stay in our rustic Sundance and Halfway Lodges. Call 403-762-4551 for a free brochure.

**Guest Ranch / Dude**

## BIG BAR GUEST RANCH

Box 27 Jesmond, Clinton, British Columbia, V0K 1K0
Tel/Fax: 604-459-2333
*Contact: Nancy Vickery*

**Open all year** • Western tack • 50 horses • Appaloosa, Palomino, Arabians and mixed breeds • Trail riding 2 rides daily, all day rides • "City Slicker" pack trips – 5 days and 6 nights • All skill levels • Lessons • Gymkhana • Guest capacity 60 • Hot tub • Fireside lounge • Billiards room • Game and video room • Canoeing • Fishing • Gold-panning • Winter sports – cross country skiing, ice fishing, sleigh rides, special Christmas package • Licensed dining room • Rail, bus and airport transfers • Member: B.C Assoc. of Guest Ranchers Assoc., Cariboo Tourist Assoc.

Big Bar Guest Ranch is situated in an area of rolling hills, mountains and meadows which provide our guests with a spectacular and challenging riding area. We provide riding experiences for the novice to advanced rider. Our pack trips take you over Big Bar Mountain and down into the awe inspiring Fraser Canyon. Accommodations are in a two story guest house, log cottages with wood burning stoves and authentic Tepees. After an active day of riding, fishing, hiking, canoeing, gold panning, bird watching and eating our gourmet home style ranch meals, relax with a game of billiards, a hot tub under the stars or a good book in the lounge. See you at the Big Bar.

Guest Ranch / Dude

## CIRCLE H MOUNTAIN LODGE

PO Box 7, Jesmond, BC V0K 1K0
Tel/Fax: 604-459-2565
E mail: circle_h@mindlink.bc.ca
{3086 Babich Street, Abbotsford, BC V2S 5H7 – Tel: 604-850-1873}
{indicates winter address – October to May}
*Contact: Mitch / Daphne Henselwood*

**Open May 15 to Oct. 15** • Western tack • 20 horses • Mountain cayoose horses • Guided trail riding - 2 times a day, all day rides 2 times a week • All skill levels accommodated • Fishing • Hiking • Guest capacity 16 • Memberships: British Columbia Guest Ranch Association, Cariboo Tourist Assoc. • Nearest airport is Kamloops or Vancouver

Circle H Mountain Lodge is a small guest ranch situated 5,000 feet up in the Limestone Mountains of the southern Cariboo in British Columbia. The main lodge has a guest wing containing five bedrooms and shared bathrooms. There are also four log cabins, small and cozy with wood stoves for the chilly mountain nights. The huge living room is a comfortable place to relax with no TV to mar the peacefulness! Dining takes place around a long table seating 20 and your hosts pride themselves on their excellent meals. Our riding program includes two daily rides and twice a week all-day rides with picnic lunches and spectacular mountain-top views.

**Guest Ranch / Dude**

## THREE BAR CATTLE AND GUEST RANCH

SS 3 Site 19-62C, Cranbrook, British Columbia V1C 6H3
Tel: 604-426-5230 Fax: 604-426-8240
*Contact: Reservations*

**Open May to Sept.** • Western tack • 100 Quarter horses • All skill levels • Lessons included • Indoor and outdoor riding arena • Guest capacity 40 • Tennis • Indoor swimming • Hot tub • (Fly) fishing • Guided hiking • River rafting • Member: Dude Ranchers' Assoc., BC Guest Ranchers Assn.

**Point to Point / Cottage to cottage**

## AU JAL A CHEVAL, INC

82, rang X11
Auclair, Quebec G0L 1A0
Tel: 418-899-6635
*Contact: Huguette Major*

**Open May to Oct.** • Western tack • 17 horses • Canadian stock, Quarter horses • 5 hours each day • Capacity 10 • Minimum age 12 • All skill levels • Point to point – weekend rides, 3 and 5 day rides • Customized trips for 6 riders or more • 3 hour drive from Quebec

*The Most Beautiful Vacation on Horseback*

Discover the grandeur of our 150 miles of trails through the lakes, mountains and rivers of the Northern Appalachians in the province of Quebec, Canada. Enjoy a different cottage every night and hearty meals served by our attentive staff. A thrilling ride in the heart of nature for everyone who loves horses and freedom. We breed our own horses. "Montagnard," "Altesse," "Arabesque" and "Alliance," born last August, add to our herd of 17 adults. We are impatiently waiting for the birth of 6 others this coming summer. Come discover the spirit. Our horses love the trail, are in great shape and are assigned according to ability and preference. Brochures in English and French.

**Point to Point / Inn to inn style**

## LA FERME DU JOUAL VAIR

Becancour, Quebec, G0L 2S0 Canada
Tel: 819-297-2107 Fax: 819-297-2106
*Contact: Bernard Giles*

**Open May to Nov.** • Western tack • 40 horses • Appaloosa, Quarter horses • All skill levels • Team penning • 2, 3 and 5 day rides • St. Laurence • 5 day Appalachian Mountain ride • Riders stay at lodges, B&B and farmhouses • Facility for clients' horses

Discover the unique flavor and color of Quebec country. Welcome to our ranch, known internationally for its hospitality, excellent food and wonderful atmosphere. Our horses will take you a magical way through maple and pine forests, over sand dunes and across the rivers. We offer you unforgettable 2, 3 and 5 day adventure trips. You might also wish to play cowboy with cattle and try some team-penning. We have horses suitable for all riders, experienced or not. We have enjoyed riding with people since 1969. The ranch is conveniently located between Montreal and Quebec City and we will be pleased to help you plan a tour before or after your ride.

**Point to Point / Camping – Lodges / Residential Riding Center**

## RANCH MASSIF DU SUD

149 Route du Massif du Sud
St. Philemon, Bellechasse, Quebec G0R 4A0, Canada
Tel: 418-469-2900 Tel: 418-883-2224 Fax: 418-883-2225
*Contact: Raymonde Garant*

**Open all year** • Western tack • 30 horses • Mix of breeds • 5 day and customized camping trips • Average saddle time – 6 hours • Ride capacity 20 • Hunting trips in season • Gold panning • Fishing • B&B opportunities • 1 hour drive from Quebec City

Start your conquest of the Parc riding through enchanted landscapes in the land of cowboys and gold prospectors. You will follow the trail of bears and deer that will lead you to the "GATES of HELL," going through streams and leading you to the Sugar Cabin (in the land of maple syrup). You will travel through unbeaten paths and you will be invited to follow the "gold rush." Accommodations are in gold prospectors' camps, chalets, country houses and bunkhouses. The starry evenings by the campfire will create some unforgettable memories. Experience Indian rituals and the life of Quebec's cowboys. The meals are delicious and always enhanced by our local and excellent maple syrup. Only 1 hour from Quebec City.

**Wilderness Lodge / Pack trips**

## MAJESTIC MOUNTAIN ALASKAN ADVENTURES, INC.

PO Box 87, Depart CT, Glennallen, Alaska 99588
Tel: 907-822-7306
*Contact: Jeff / Cyndi Chadd*

**Open June 1 to August 1** • Western tack • 15 Mountain Horses • All skill levels • Daily rides • 3, 4 and 5 day customized pack trips • 6 hours riding each day • 5 day fishing trips – king and red salmon, dolly varden, grayling and lake trout • Gold panning • Shooting • Fishing • Hiking • Bird watching • Sauna • Guest capacity 4 to 6

Our wilderness camp is accessible only by small float plane and horseback. It is Alaska at its wildest! See eagles, moose, bears, wolves and Dall sheep. Our family-run remote camp, located in the Chugach Mountains, consists of a hand-crafted lodge which houses the kitchen, dining room and lounging area, private guest cabins and a sauna/shower house. Enjoy hearty home cooked meals and fresh baked goods. Your adventure opportunities are limitless, safe and entirely designed for your pleasure. You can ride out from our camp every day during your stay, aided by our capable staff, or opt for a customized packtrip on reliable, sure-footed horses. Fishing enthusiasts can enjoy fishing for king salmon on secluded streams reached by horseback or foot.

Cattle Ranch

## NORTHLAND RANCH RESORT

PO Box 2376, Kodiak, AK 99615
Tel: 907-486-5578

**Open mid May to Nov.** • Western tack • 45 Quarter horses • Trail riding from ranch • Pack trips up to 5 days • All skill levels • Guest capacity 20 • Children 5 and older can go trail riding • Riding and horse care lessons • Fishing (five species of salmon and two species of trout) • Wildlife watching • Barbecue • Housebar • Member: Alaska Farmers and Stock Growers, Highland Breeders Assoc., Kodiak Chamber of Commerce, Kodiak Convention and Visitors Bureau and Kodiak Soil and Water Conservation Service

Grab your chance and spend some time on a large working ranch in one of the most beautiful locations in the world! Enjoy great horseback riding, Alaska's amazing wilderness and unique fishing opportunities for salmon and trout. Spend some quiet hours in contemplation and wildlife watching for mountain goats, whales, eagles and maybe you will see on of the world's giant bears – a Kodiak bear! We offer you a real ranch experience on our 30,000 plus acres. We are located on the blue Pacific Ocean between rugged mountains and grasslands. Come and we will be happy to show you our piece of Alaska. Call or write for more information.

**Outfitter**

## WOLF POINT RANCH

Denali Wilderness Outfitters, Inc.
PO Box 127, Cantwell, AK 99729
Tel: 800-367-8173 Tel/Fax: 907-768-2620
*Contact: Kirk Martakis*

**Open June to Aug.** (Riding vacations) • 13 Horses • Saddle horses • Four and six day pack trips • All skill levels • Limit 6 to a ride • Fishing – Graylings (stream) and Lake Trout • Open Spring and Fall • Guided hunts • Open Feb. to April • Snowmobiling, Dog sled trips

Wolf Point Ranch, located in Denali National Park's backyard, provides year round full service wilderness experience. Our summer rides into Denali offer the opportunity to enjoy the majesty of the Alaskan wilderness. You will see a great variety of wildlife on land and in the air. The fishing is fantastic. The four and six day trips may be combined. Whether experiencing our summer riding, our spring and fall hunts or our winter dog sled (or snow mobile) adventure, you will encounter an experienced staff, a high level of camp comforts and detailed attention to health and safety in our remote, pristine wilderness.

**Guest Ranch / Cattle**

## GRAPEVINE CANYON RANCH

PO Box 302, Dept. WWRV, Pearce, AZ 85625
Tel: 800-245-9202 Tel: 520-826-3185 Fax: 520-826-3636
E-mail: egrapevine@earthlink.net
*Contact: Bonnie St. Clair, Nona Vee Myer*

**Open all year** • Western Saddle • 60 Horses • Quarter horses • Seasonal cattle work • 3 to 6 hours a day riding • All skill levels • Riding lessons • Weekly horsemanship clinics • Cowboy clinics • Guest Capacity of 30 • Heated pool • Hot tub • Guests 12 years and older • Member: Dude Ranchers' Assoc., AZ Dude Ranch Assoc.

*Come spend unhurried time .........*

This secluded guest and working cattle ranch specializes in the best of friendly, personal service. Guests are housed in well appointed, widely spaced cabins or casita suites with sundecks offering magnificent views of the rugged Dragoon Mountains or distant Chiricahuas. We have alert and responsive horses for all levels of riding skill and offer trail riding on scenic mountain trails, riding lessons, horsemanship seminars, reining clinics, team penning and cowboy clinics where you can learn roping, sorting, driving cattle and other cowboy skills. We are in historic Apache country, near legendary Tombstone, Old Mexico and other great sightseeing and shopping destinations. And we offer the best of country cooking served in our private dining room.

*Discover How the West Was Once....*
*and still is, at Grapevine Canyon Ranch.*

**Guest Ranch / Cattle**

## HORSESHOE RANCH ON BLOODY BASIN ROAD

HCR 34, Box 5005 – WWRV, Mayer, AZ 86333
Tel: 520-632-8813 Fax: 520-632-8813
*Contact: Reservations*

**Open year round** • Western tack • 42 Ranch horses • Not for beginning or unfit riders • Roping instruction • Ring for team penning • Adults and teens only • Solo guests our specialty • Guest capacity of 12 • Member: Dude Ranchers' Assoc. and AZ Dude Ranch Assoc.

1700 head of cattle graze on 100 square miles of mesas, canyons and mountains in the beautiful snow-free Arizona high country at an altitude of 3000 to 5800 feet. Saddle up and help search, gather, drive, sort, rope, brand, dehorn and doctor... just the way it's been done on the Horseshoe Ranch for more than 100 years. What you don't know, the cowboys will teach you. After the dust, noise and excitement of a day working cattle, settle into the comfort of a large private bedroom with bath in a modern ranch home. Then join the whole ranch family at one giant table to enjoy abundant good food and conversation that relives the day on the range. Come share the real western ranch life! One hour north of Phoenix on the way to Sedona and the Grand Canyon.

KAY EL BAR
GUEST RANCH
SINCE 1926

**Guest Ranch / Dude**

## KAY EL BAR RANCH

PO Box 2480, Wickenburg, AZ 85358
Tel: 520-684-7593
*Contact: Jane Nash*

**Open Oct. 15 to May 1** • Western saddles • 25 grade and registered Quarter horses • All skill levels • Two 2-hour rides daily • One ride Sunday • Heated pool • Horseshoes, ping pong, croquet • Member Dude Ranchers' Assoc., AZ Dude Ranch Assoc.

Welcome to our cozy, casual family ranch and spectacular riding trails. Our riding program consists of two 2-hour rides each day except Sundays and holidays, when only one ride is available. Rides are separated by skill level. We ride through beautiful Arizona mid-Sonoran desert country ringed by the Bradshaw Mountains. Enjoy hearty, delicious meals and relax at our heated pool and our comfortable lodge room with an inviting fireplace and bar. Nearby golf, the historic Western town of Wickenburg and Phoenix are some of the options for a day off from ranching.

**Guest Ranch / Dude**

## LAZY K BAR RANCH

8401 N. Scenic Drive, Tucson, AZ 85743
Tel: 800-321-7018 Tel: 520-744-3050 Fax: 520-744-7628
E Mail: lazyk@theriver.com
Web: http//mmm.arizonaguide.com/Lazy.K
*Contact: Carol Moore*

**Open year round** • Western tack • 60 horses • Quarter horses • All skill levels • Walk and lope rides twice daily, except Sunday • Team penning • Children must be 6 or older for trail rides • Guest capacity 50 to 60 • Two lighted tennis courts • Heated pool • Outdoor spa • Cookouts • Hayrides • C/W dancing • Nature programs • Member: Dude Ranchers' Assoc., AZ Dude Ranch Assoc.

The Lazy K is a small, authentic western ranch nestled in the Tucson Mountains. Its informal atmosphere and friendly nature make the ranch perfect for families, couples, singles and small corporate meetings. Our nightly rate includes lodging, all meals, horseback riding twice daily, except on Sunday, and courtesy airport transfers. There are a total of 23 rooms, all with individual heat/air and full bath. A heated pool, outdoor spa and two lighted tennis courts are a few of the ranch amenities. We offer walking and loping rides and team penning. Riding lessons, moonlight rides and sunrise rides are available at an additional charge.

*See Color Photo Page 118*

**Guest Ranch / Dude**

## WHITE STALLION RANCH

9251 W. Twin Peaks Rd., Dept. WWRV,Tucson, AZ 85743
Tel: 520-297-0252 Tel: 800-782-5546 Fax: 520-744-2786
*Contact: True Family*

**Open Oct. 1 to May 31** • Western tack • 80 horses • Many Quarter horses • 3 to 4 rides each day • No riding on Sunday • 4 to 7 hours in saddle each day • Team penning • Weekly show rodeo • Guest capacity of 75 • Heated swimming pool • Tennis • Hot Tub • Children's petting zoo • Member: AZ Dude Ranch Assoc., Dude Ranchers' Assoc.

This charming, informal ranch gives you a true feeling of the Old West. Only here can you find 3,000 acres of wide open land at the foot of the beautiful Tucson Mountains. Here ranch informality is blended perfectly with the comforts of a top resort. Enjoy the Western style horseback riding with the wranglers, fine horses and scores of scenic trails. Facilities to enjoy are the heated pool, hot tub, tennis and many more. The ranch is noted for delicious meals, cookouts, breakfast rides, hayrides and rodeos. Please call or write for more information.

Outfitter

## DON DONNELLY HORSEBACK VACATIONS

6010 S. King Rd., Dept. CT, Gold Canyon, AZ 85219
Tel: 602-982-7822 Tel: 800-346-4403 Fax: 602-982-8795
*Contact: Mary Lou*

**Open March through Nov.** (for trips) • Riding stables open all year • 50 horses • Quarter horses • 5, 7 and 8 day pack trips – base camp style • Average saddle time – 6 to 8 hours • Trips to Monument Valley, White Mountains, San Rafael Valley, Superstition Wilderness • All skill levels • Children and older

We offer unique vacation packages for those who want a western experience but still want some of the comforts not usually found on pack trips. We provide our guests with large tents, cots, fabulous western cooking and hot showers. Arizona is a land that is extremely diverse, with mountains, deserts and rolling grass lands. One of our most popular destinations is Monument Valley. This ride is a favorite with everyone world wide. We are continually scouting new locations to insure that our guests keep coming back for more exciting adventures on horseback. Call Don Donnelly Horseback Vacations at 1-800-346-4403.

PHOTO: WALTER MEAD

Inn

## HOWARD CREEK RANCH

40501 North Hwy. One, PO Box 121, Westport, CA 95488
Tel: 707-964-6725 Fax: 707-964-6725 (Call first )
*Contact: Reservations*

**Open all year** • (English or Western riding at neighboring Ricochet Ridge Stable – 50 horses) • Orlov Crosses, Akhal-Teke, Arabians, Thoroughbreds, Appaloosa • Jumping – dressage • Trail riding • Adults only • Inn capacity 22 • Hot tub • Sauna • German masseuse • Heated pool • English, German, Spanish, Italian and Dutch spoken

Howard Creek Ranch is a historic 40 acre oceanfront farm bordered by miles of beach and mountains near a 60 mile long wilderness. The ranch offers farm animals, flower gardens, fireplaces, wood stoves, a 75 foot swinging foot bridge over Howard Creek, a hot tub, sauna and German masseuse. Accommodations include cabins, suites and rooms furnished with antiques, large comfortable beds and handmade quilts with views of the ocean, mountains, creek or gardens. Visit the gigantic redwoods, take the famous Skunk Train, shop in the village of Mendocino, go horseback riding on the beach and enjoy our spectacular, scenic area.

English or Western enthusiasts will enjoy riding for miles along Pacific beaches, through a working cattle ranch and up to the coastal mountain range, richly covered with towering conifers, offering views that stretch to eternity. Although Howard Creek Ranch has its own farm animals, none of the riding horses reside on the property. All riding is conducted by Ricochet Ridge Stables, a separate business, owned and operated by Lari Shea, winner of the prestigious Tevis Cup 100 Mile Endurance race. Ricochet's private rides require advance reservations. Her horses excel on the trail and in dressage and jumping.

**Guest Ranch / Cattle**

## HUNEWILL GUEST RANCH

PO Box 368, CT, Bridgeport, CA 93517
Tel: 619- 932-7462 Tel: 702-465-2201
*Contact: Betty / Jennifer*

**Open May 15 to Oct. 1** • Western saddles • 130 Horses • Mixed breeds • 5 hours a day riding • Morning and afternoon rides • All skill levels • Guest capacity 45 • Fishing • Hiking in Sierras • Facility for clients' horses • Cattle drives • Working cattle ranch • Founded 1861 • Special children's program • Family owned, 6th generation • Member: Dude Ranchers' Assoc.

Hunewill Ranch is situated in the lovely Bridgeport Valley, Mono County, California, 6500 feet above sea level, in the heart of the eastern Sierra. We are a family owned and operated working cattle ranch since 1861. You won't want to go home. Our ranch house built in 1880 is a fine example of Victorian architecture. Horseback riding is our specialty. We have 130 horses, one just right for you. Children's riding program, breathtaking mountain scenery, hay rides, cattle work, fall color ride, 5 day cattle drive and more are all part of the fun. Call or write for free color brochures.

**Outfitter**

## McGEE CREEK PACK STATION

Rt 1, Box 162, Dept. WWV,
Mammoth Lakes, CA 93546
Tel: 619-935-4324 Tel: 800-854-7407 Fax: 619-878-2207 (winter tel)
*Contact: Jennifer / Lee Roeser*

**Open May 25 to Sept. 30** • Western tack • Daily rides • Customized pack trips 1 to 7 days • Average saddle time of 3 hours • Cattle roundups • Horsedrives • Wagon train trips • All skill levels • Ages 6 and older • Member: Eastern High Sierra Packers Assoc.

Located ten miles south of Mammoth Lakes in California's spectacular Eastern High Sierra, we offer personalized vacations for families and groups to the secluded regions of John Muir Wilderness. In operation for more than 25 years, our dependable, organized Spot trip services provide the ideal vacation for families and sportsmen alike. From daily trail rides to 6 day all-inclusive excursions, we have the vacation package for you. We also offer Death Valley Wagon Trains, movie location wagon tours and trail rides in the Alabama Hills, a Professional Wilderness Packing School and special events for groups. We invite you to write or call for brochures, maps and information.

**Point to Point / Inn to Inn**

## LARI SHEA'S RICOCHET RIDGE RANCH

24201 North Highway One, Fort Bragg, CA 95437
Tel: 1-888-TREK-RRR (1-888-873-5777) Tel: 707-964-7669
Tel/Fax: 707-964-9669 (office)
Web site: http://www.horse-vacation.com
E-mail: larishea@horse-vacation.com

**Open year round** • Western and English • 50 horses • Arabian, Thoroughbred, Appaloosa, Akhal Teke, Orlov crosses • May to Oct. 6 day Redwood Coast Beach and Forest Ride • June 3 to 9 Distance Riding and Sport Horse Seminar • Winter 97 horsetrek to Australia • Guest capacity 2 to 20 • Lessons available • All skill levels

Redwood Coast Beach & Forest Horse Trek Adventures. Canter deserted beaches, ride the bluffs while the Pacific crashes against rocks far below, meander on mossy trails in the Redwood Forest or ride through a working cattle ranch onto a coastal mountain range. Lodge at historic Mendocino hotel and two unique B&B inns by the ocean. Elegant dining, fine wines, delightful hot tubs under the stars and entertainment nightly by acclaimed musicians. Lari Shea, winner of the prestigious Tevis Cup 100 Mile Endurance Race, leads all 6 night treks and the distance training seminar culminating in a 25 to 50 mile Endurance Ride. All experience levels – English and Western – Quality Horses. Please ask about riding vacations to Australia/Fiji, France and India.

**Residential Riding Center**

## ADVENTURES ON HORSEBACK

32628 Endeavor Way, Union City, CA 94587
Tel: 510-487-9001
*Contact: Donna Synder-Smith*

**Open April through Oct.** • English, Endurance saddles • Mustangs (formerly wild horses adopted from BLM) • 5 day endurance riding holiday • 5 day instruction holiday featuring centered riding techniques • 5 day trail riding holiday • Only instructional holiday open to all skill levels • Guest capacity 2 to 6 • Indoor riding • Facilities for clients' horses • Member: AERC, ARICP, AHSA

At the edge of the exciting city of San Francisco, this touring company offers the unique opportunity to ride big, beautiful, formerly wild Mustangs! Guests may explore trails in wilderness reserves, improve skills by learning centered riding techniques from national award winning coach Donna Synder-Smith or try the exciting sport of endurance riding on one of Donna's experienced horses. Guests stay in a lovely bed and breakfast, furnished with antiques, offering private baths and lots of atmosphere. The food is diverse, fun and very good.

**Resort**

## THE ALISAL GUEST RANCH & RESORT

1054 Alisal Road, Solvang, CA 93463
Tel: 800-425-4725 Tel: 805-688-6411 Fax: 805-688-2510
*Contact: Reservations*

**Open year round** • Western tack • 60 quarter horses • Riding lessons • All skill levels • Rodeo • Special children's program • Two golf courses on property • Tennis • Swimming • Hot tub • Fishing • Boating • Lake on property • 150 guest capacity

The Alisal Guest Ranch and Resort is a working cattle ranch and full service resort, privately owned and operated since 1946. A 10,000 acre ranch with 73 guest rooms offers a high level of accommodation. Facilities include two 18 hole championship golf courses, seven tennis courts, a 96 acre fishing/boating lake, horseback riding over miles of scenic trails, swimming pool, a variety of children's activities, rodeos, barbecues, wine maker dinners and meeting facilities for 200 delegates. Located outside Solvang, approximately 2 hours from Los Angeles and 40 minutes north of Santa Barbara. From November to March 31 and midweek during September, October, April and May (excluding holidays), the room rates include unlimited golf, tennis, horseback riding and lake activities.

**Cattle Drives / Point to Point**

## KIRKWELL CATTLE COMPANY

7116 County Rd. U, Pritchett, CO 81064
Tel: 719-523-4422 Tel: 719-523-6496 (Dean) Tel: 719-324-9292 (Wes)
*Contact: Dean Ormiston, Wes McKinley*

**Open May through Oct.** • Western saddles • 20 Quarter horses • Cattle drives – 5 days • Rough Rider rides – 5 days • Special customized wagon train supported rides • Base camps • Skill level varies with trip • Cowboy poetry and singing

Kirkwell Cattle Company and Dean and Wes, the two Colorado cowboys who run it, like to provide a genuine cowboy experience. The lower plateau land that characterizes the corner of Colorado that kisses Oklahoma and New Mexico lets you enjoy some hard riding when and if you want it. Wagon supported trips and base camps let you enjoy a well supplied rest for your ride weary bones. Their scheduled trips begin in May with a wagon train supported trip. Spring and fall brings on some of the best cattle driving trips in the country and October brings a five day Rough-Rider trip. Groups seeking their own style cowboy experience should give a holler.

**Guest Ranch / Dude**

## BAR LAZY J GUEST RANCH

PO Box N, Parshall, CO 80468
Tel: 970-725-3437 Tel: 800-396-6279 Fax: 970-725-3437
*Contact: Jerry / Cheri Helmicki*

**Open May to Oct** • Western saddles • 60 horses • Quarters, Appaloosas, Arabians • All skill levels • Lessons available • Guest capacity 38 • Heated pool • Sauna • Fly fishing • Special children's program • Nearby golf and tennis and whitewater rafting • Member: Dude Ranchers' Assoc., Colorado Dude & Guest Ranch Assoc.

Colorado's oldest continuously operating guest ranch. Located 105 northwest of Denver; altitude 7500 ft. Nestled in a peaceful valley along the beautiful Colorado river. GOLD MEDAL fishing. We offer great horseback riding for all levels. Jeep rides, river rafting, mountain biking, sightseeing van trips to nearby Rocky Mountain National Park. Warm Western hospitality and delicious home cooking served in our historic lodge. Daily children's program, evening entertainment, recreation barn, heated swimming pool and jacuzzi. Listen to the river rush by in your private cabin. We are an ideal place for a family vacation with plenty to do for all members of the family.

**Guest Ranch / Dude**

## C LAZY U RANCH

PO Box 379 – WWRV, Granby, CO 80466
Tel: 970-887-3344 Fax: 970-887-3917
*Contact: Reservations*

**Open mid May to Oct. and mid Dec. through March** • Western tack • 165 horses • Quarter horses • Two 2 hour rides per day – summer season • Two 1 hour rides – winter season • Buck Brannaman's Fall horsemanship and cow clinics • Adults only – Fall season • Swimming • Sauna • Fishing • Shooting • Tennis • Cross-country and downhill skiing in season

**Guest Ranch / Cattle**

## COLORADO RANCH CONNECTION, INC.

8464 Old San Isabel Road, Rye, CO 81069
Tel/Fax: 719-489-2266
*Contact: Shannon / Roy Christenson*

**May through Sept.** • Working ranch vacations, western style • Family operated • Capacity 6 to 8 • Excellent ranch quarter horses • Unlimited riding • Riding instruction • Cattle work •All skill levels • Oct. and Nov. – Private land deer, elk, bear and turkey hunts • Some off season activity – Feb. through April

**Guest Ranch / Dude**

## HARMELS GUEST RANCH

PO Box 399 W, Almont, CO 81210
Tel: 970-641-1740 Tel: 800-235-3402 Fax: 970-641-1944
*Contact: Brad Milner*

**Open mid May to Sept. 30** • Western tack • 55 – 60 horses • Pleasure • saddle horses • Overnight pack trips • All skill levels • Swimming • Fishing • Shooting • Whitewater rafting • Mountain biking • Special children's programs • Square dancing • Entertainment • Game room • Gift shop • Hayrides • Member: CO and Guest Ranch Assoc.

**Guest Ranch / Cattle**

## COLORADO GUEST RANCH / CHIPETA RANCH

1938 Hwy. 133, Dept. CT, Paonia, CO 81428
Tel: 970-929-6260 Tel: 800-521-4055 Fax: 970-929-6250
*Contact: Reservations*

**Open all year** • Western saddles • 30 horses • Appaloosa, Quarter horse, Stock horses • Cattle round-up • 1, 5 and 7 day pack trips • Hourly, half day, all day rides • Ranch stays • Guest capacity of 32 • Hunting in season – archery, muzzle loading, rifle – bear, elk, mule deer, mountain lion • 15 "Ropins" • 3 Rodeos • Wild West Poker Run • Cowboy Golf Classic • Cowboy Mountain horse races • 3 country concerts • Fishing • Member: CO Outfitters & Guide Assoc – Lic #1463

Let us show you Colorado's Majestic Mountains, reality and the Cowboy life, ride and rope, laugh and joke all year round. Thrilling outdoor experiences combine the old west with the simple comforts of the 20th century. Let our experienced guides and wranglers show you our wilderness resort. 4,000 acres of private land with an additional 16,000 acres of leased government land. Wildlife abounds like elk, mule deer, mountain lions, bears, song birds and birds of prey, from the river bottom at 5,900 feet to the mountain top at 9,000 feet. Family activities, rodeos, arena events and casual ranch living.

**Guest Ranch / Dude**

## COLORADO TRAILS RANCH

12161 County Road 240, Dept. CT, Durango, CO 81301
Tel: 800-323-DUDE Tel: 970-247-5055 Fax: 970-385-7372
E-Mail: Co T Ranch@aol.com.
*Contact: Jeanne Ross*

**Open June to mid-Sept.** • Western saddle • 100 horses • Quarter, Morgans, Arabian, TB, Belgium • Lessons • Rides divided by skill level • Special children's program • Special adult weeks – 6/2, 8/25, 9/1, 9/8 • Guest capacity of 65 • Swimming • Tennis • Fishing • Riflery • Archery • Trap shooting • Nearby golf and river rafting • Guided trips to Mesa Verde Nat'l Park • Evening programs • Member: CO Dude & Guest Ranch Assoc., Dude Ranchers' Assoc., Amer. Riding Instruction Cert. Pro. (ARICP)

Since 1960. Our riding program is nationally acclaimed. Certified riding instructors and superbly trained horses provide an exciting, educational and safe riding experience for all levels of riders. We ride on spectacular terrain in the San Juan Mountains. When you're not on a horse, you can enjoy tennis, swimming, shooting sports, water skiing, river rafting, fishing, evening programs and more. The kids have the time of their lives in three groups with full-time counselors. To round out your vacation with us, we have squeaky clean cabins, delicious home cooking and baking, top facilities and a great staff. You'll love it.

**Guest Ranch / Dude**

## DROWSY WATER RANCH

PO Box 147, WRV, Granby, CO 80446
Tel: 800-845-2292 (reservations) Tel: 970-725-3456
Fax: 970-725-3611
*Contact: Ken / Randy Sue Fosha*

**Open June to mid-Sept.** • Western tack • Lessons available • 100 head of horses • Paints and Quarter horses • Children's program • Adults only in Sept. • Swimming • Hot tub • Capacity – 55 guests • Member: CO Dude & Guest Ranch Assoc., Dude Ranchers' Assoc., Mobil Guide, Licensed outfitter #277

Our famous 600-acre ranch borders back country, giving you a secluded family paradise. Our skilled wranglers instruct beginners through advanced riders on scenic and loping rides, breakfast, half and all day rides. Our supervised children's program will keep children ages 6 to 13 having fun all week. Competent counselors will entertain children 5 and younger. Fishing, overnight pack trip, rafting and 4 x 4 rides. Golf and tennis nearby. Delicious family style, all you can eat meals, steaks fries, cookouts, homemade breads and desserts. Newly remodeled comfortable log cabin or lodge accommodations. Weekly American plan includes horses. Family plan rates. Non-riders, early and late season discounts. See outfitters section.

**Guest Ranch / Dude / Resort**

## WIT'S END GUEST AND RESORT RANCH

254 C.R. 500 CT, Bayfield, CO 81122
Tel: 970-884-4113 Fax: 970-884-3261 – summer
Tel: 602-263-0000 Fax: 602-234-0298 – winter
*Contact: Jen Stringfellow*

**Open May 1 to Oct. 20** • Open year round for groups • Western tack • 106 quarter horses • Full riding program • 3 to 21 day pack trips – customized • Weekly and seasonal cattle drive • Hunting in season • Full children's summer program • Adults only after Labor Day• Tennis • Heated swimming pool • Mountain bikes • Hot tubs • Fly fishing • Lake swimming • Motor tours • 3 Diamond AAA, 3 star Mobil, 4 star Reeds, Superior 1st class Hotel Guide • Membership: AQHA, Assoc. Member: Dude Ranchers' Assoc., CO Outfitter's & Guide Assoc. – License number 1004

*WELCOME TO WIT'S END GUEST AND RESORT RANCH*

You are no longer at your Wit's End, you are now at our Wit's End for a week of fun and relaxation. Nestled at the edge of the San Juan Mountains in the 2,000,000 acre San Juan National Forest in southwestern Colorado, the Vallecito Lake Valley is proof positive that the "Old West" lives on. Your dreams of the West are about to come true when you breathe in that clean mountain air, feast your eyes on blankets of wild flowers and listen to musical brooks as they meander and babble along. Surrounded by 12,000 to 14,000 foot peaks, snow capped until mid July, the mountains here scrape the sky. During your visit, you'll be "corralled" at the rustic Wit's End Guest and Resort Ranch where city slickers become cowboys overnight and log cabins turn into rustic fantasies perched at the edge of wilderness. Vestiges of the past resound everywhere at the 1860 historic "Wit's End Ranch," sprawled adjacent to 575,000 acres of wilderness, 28 miles from Durango, Colorado. Time seems to stand still at Wit's End, but you'll be able to do as much or as little as you want.
Wit's End has a myriad of activities from which to choose. Your surroundings will include 100 or more horses, miles of trail riding, wilderness hikes, tennis, hot tubs, a 50 foot heated pool, fishing, pack trips, rivers, a pond, a large lake with 22 miles of shoreline, nature trail hiking, cycling and 4 wheel drive excursions...all in spectacular scenic beauty. Your log cabin comes equipped with down comforters, balloon drapes, berber carpeting, a stone fireplace, full kitchen

furnishings and decor for the most discriminating tastes. Log decks and hand hewn porch swings are included in a magnificent hand hewn structure containing the main dining area, gathering and recreational area, a full bar and the crystal mirrors from the 1836 Crystal Palace of London. The ranch provides a great children's and teens' program allowing you to spend time with and time without the kids. Overnight camps, riding, fishing and games keep them busy while the adults enjoy 4 nights of romantic fine dining, great comradeship with the owners, family and staff. We eat outside 3 nights a week. Western Cookouts, arena events and Western two stepping are all part of the fun. Come on over, the whole gang is looking forward to meeting you.

*See Color Photo Pages 122–127*

Outfitter

## CAPITOL PEAK OUTFITTERS, INC.

0554 Valley Rd., Carbondale, CO 81623
Tel: 970-963-0211 Fax: 970-963-0497
*Contact: Sandy / Steve Rieser*

**Open May through Sept.** • Riding holidays • Western tack • 75 saddle and pack horses • 1 to 7 day wilderness pack trips • Wall tent base camps • Drop Camps • Daily hour, half and full day rides • Aug. 31 to Nov. 10 – hunting • Archery, muzzle loading and rifle seasons for elk and deer • Special full day fishing excursions • Member: CO Outfitters & Guide Assoc., License # 741, White River National Forest

We offer a full range of horseback opportunities from hourly rides to all expense wilderness pack trips and fully guided hunting and fishing expeditions. We are located near the resort town of Aspen, Colorado. Our trips center in the Maroon Bells/Snowmass Wilderness, a setting unsurpassed with 14,000 foot peaks, mountain lakes, wildflowers and breathtaking panoramas. Our goal is to leave you with great memories of the scenic, pristine and enchanting countryside in the Rockies, the delicious home cooked meals shared with good friends and our friendly, professional and hardworking staff and the memory of your horse as a trustworthy companion that got you there and back safely.

**Outfitter**

## DOUBLE DIAMOND

PO Box 2-WWRV, Meredith, CO 81642
Tel/Fax: 970-927-3404
*Contact: Jack or Joan Wheeler*
Licensed guide/outfitter for White River National Forest, State Reg.# 637

**Open all year** • Western tack • 18 Mountain horses, 10 mules • Beginners welcome • Scenic high country trails • Pack trips • Swimming • Hot tub • Fishing • Shooting • Hunting trips – guided, one on one, drop camps and full service camps • Member: CO Outfitters & Guide Assoc.

Enjoy 3 to 5 day full service working ranch vacations in majestic Frying Pan Valley. Throw away your workaday blues and be a ranch hand for a week or relax and enjoy the horses, hot tub and nature. Bed and breakfast opportunities are possible at ranchhouse or wilderness cabins. Enjoy 3 to 5 day customized pack trips at picturesque comfortable high-mountain tent camps or progressive 5 day pack trips on sure-footed mountain horses and mules. Educational "leave no trace trips," working eco trip for USFS projects and hunting and fishing packages year round.

**Outfitter**

## MARVINE AND LUNNEY OUTFITTERS

PO Box 569,WWRV, Meeker, CO 81641
Tel: 970-878-4320 Tel: 800-371-6042 Fax: 970-878-4320
*Contact: Brett J. Harvey, CO outfitters # 1576, #1394 operating Routt and White River Nat'l Forest, Flat Tops Wilderness area*

**Open May 15 to Nov. 15** • Western tack • 30 quarter horses • Beginners welcome • Varying length vacations • Pack trips • Drop camps – main luxury camps – cabin • (Fly) fishing – shooting – private ranch hunts – mule deer and elk by horse or 4 WD • Fly fishing and riding lessons • Member: Rocky Mt. Elk Foundation, CO Outfitters & Guide Assoc.

Our focus is to provide a package that serves our clients interests and to develop an itinerary that entertains these interests and desires. You may stay at our ranch cabin or comfortable main wilderness camps or enjoy your own drop camps or progressive pack trips through the wilderness. The packages can be arranged to emphasize fly or spin-cast fishing (brook, cutthroat, rainbow and brown trout), hunting in season (mule deer and elk) or spectacular scenery, great riding and photography. Whatever trip option you choose, we provide professional, personalized guide service, while nature provides a variety of activities to enjoy.

**Outfitter**

## RAPP GUIDES & PACKERS

47 Electra Lake Rd., Dept W, Durango, CO 81301
Tel: 970-247-8923 Fax: 970-247-1255
*Contact: Anne Rapp*

**Open year round** • Extended trips May to Oct. • Western tack • 50 quarter horse types, appaloosas, mules • 5 to 8 hours average saddle time • All skill levels • 8 to 10 capacity • 3 to 6 day base camps and pack trips • Lessons • Fishing • Educational commentary • Hiking • Member: CO Outfitters & Guide Assoc., State Reg. #511, AAA rated

Jerry, Anne Rapp and the helpful experienced crew welcome you to Southwest Colorado's rugged San Juan Mountains, Weminuche Wilderness and Ute Mountain Tribal Park, home to Anasazi ruins. Base camps provide comfortable heated wall tents, a good opportunity to fish for trout and explore Anasazi historical sights. Base camps are changed weekly to avoid overuse. Pack trips average 12 miles daily. Cross high mountain passes. We offer lay over days to rest, explore and fish. Customized trips for groups of 10 to 30 riders are ideal for business groups, educational groups and larger international parties. Established in 1981, we enjoy sharing our knowledge of the area's history and look forward to hearing from you.

COME TO ONE OF SCOTLAND'S
HAYFIELD
EQUESTRIAN CENTRE:SCOTLAND
HAYFIELD
AND BE SURROUNDED BY
THE VERY BEST OF SCOTLAND

PHOTO: FIONA MELLER

"On the Seventh Day" *Equitrek, Australia*

PHOTO: KROOMBIT TOURIST PARK

Cook's Assistant *Equitrek, Australia*

*Casa De Campo, Dominican Republic*

*Lazy K Bar Ranch, Arizona*

*Hargrave Cattle and Guest Ranch, Montana*

PHOTO: LAURA OZEREDZUK

PHOTO: LAURA OZEREDZUK

*Blackwater Creek Ranch, Wyoming*

PHOTOS: LAURA OZEREDZUK

*Blackwater Creek Ranch, Wyoming*

*Wit's End Guest and Resort Ranch, Colorado*

*Wit's End Guest and Resort Ranch, Colorado*

*Wit's End Guest and Resort Ranch, Colorado*

*Wit's End Guest and Resort Ranch, Colorado*

*Wit's End Guest and Resort Ranch, Colorado*

*Wit's End Guest and Resort Ranch, Colorado*

**Outfitter**

## RED FEATHER GUIDES AND OUTFITTERS

PO Box 1044, Vail, CO 81658
Tel: 970-476-3681 (Nov. 15 – June 15)
PO Box 16, Walden, CO 80480
Tel: 970-723-4204
*Contact: Arnie Schlottman / Todd Peterson*

**Open May 25 to Oct. 15** • Western tack • 25 Quarter horses • Daily horseback rides, lunch and dinner rides • Customized pack trips • All skill levels • Fall – Guided private land and wilderness hunt – deer and elk • Cabin rentals • Sauna • Hot tub • Member: CO Outfitters & Guide Assoc., Operate under permits by CO State Forest, State Park,USFS – Routt Nat'l Forest, CO outfitters License # 666

Ride the continental divide into some of Colorado's most serene wilderness where sightings of wildlife are not uncommon. Camp at a different high country lake each night where you can hike, horseback ride, fish, take pictures or just enjoy the serenity of the wilderness. Part of the family can horseback ride while the others fly fish. We provide a full time camp cook to ensure quality meals at all times. At the main lodge, electrically heated cabins are comfortable, but rustic. We cater to clients' schedules and will set up the trip to fit their time schedule.

**Outfitter**

## SAN JUAN OUTFITTING, LLC

186 C.R. 228, WWRV, Durango, CO 81301
Tel: 970-259-6259 Fax: 970-259-2652
E-Mail: sjo@frontier.net
http: // www.hwi.com/SJO/SJOHOME.html
*Contact: Tom / Cheri Van Soelen*

**Open April to Nov.** • Western tack • 30 horses • Mustangs, Quarter horses • Pack trips – 3 to 8 days and customized • 4 to 5 hours average saddle time • Base camps and progressive trips • Fall hunts – guided, semi-guided and drop camps • Spectacular photography opportunities • Member: Rocky Mt. Elk Foundation, CO Outfitters & Guide Assoc. – CO Registration # 997

San Juan Outfitting specializes in classic western horse packtrips. We offer only high quality trips catering to small groups. Our Spring packtrips take you into the ruins of the Anasazi Indians for 3 to 4 days. Summer and fall packtrips for fishing, photography and relaxing takes you fifteen miles into the Weminuche Wilderness to a base camp at an elevation of 10,300 feet. Our High Country Lake Trip travel through portions of the Continental Divide, utilizing three different camp sites. Our Continental Divide Ride is a true adventure. Traveling approximately 100 miles at an average elevation of 12,500 feet on the Divide for eight days, we enjoy all that nature has to offer.

**Residential Learning Center / Cross-Country Jumping**

## FOX EQUESTRIAN

2000 County Road 30A, Walden, CO 80480
Tel: 800-391-4735 Fax/Tel: 970-723-4325
*Contact: Hans Henzi*

*ONLY U.S. RESORT SPECIALIZING IN CROSS-COUNTRY*

**Open end of May to end of Oct.** • 250 Cross-Country jumps from 18" to 3'9" • 20 well trained horses • Thoroughbreds, Quarter horses, Crossbreeds, Appaloosa • 220' x 300' show jumping arena with sand footing • 1,500 acre property • 20 by 60 meter indoor arena • Stubben tack, Tipperary safety vests • Guest capacity of 15 • Hiking • Biking • Fishing on ranch • With nearby Western outfitter – trail riding and guided fly fishing

Fox Equestrian was built in 1992 in a spectacular Rocky Mountain setting to enjoy cross-country jumping at its best. Enjoy our comfortable lodge with beautifully appointed rooms, gorgeous views, gourmet cuisine, spacious living room with a large fire place, bar, outdoor decks, Jacuzzi and pool room. Our specialty is getting people that are able to jump 18 inch fences safely introduced into cross-country jumping or improve their skills up to the preliminary level. The 250' jumps include all the classics of eventing like water complex, drops, steps, corners, banks, combinations and single fences. There are up to two daily rides of 2-1/2 hours each, grouped according to riding experience and always accompanied by a highly qualified staff who gives as much instruction as you wish. Private instruction available. Weekly packages with one or two rides daily, Saturday through Saturday. Minimum stay 2 days. Rebates for non-riding accompanying person. Bringing your own horse possible.Combine the best of spectacular western landscape, European hospitality and professional cross-country instruction.

Outfitter

## DROWSY WATER RANCH

PO Box 147, WWRV, Granby, CO 80446
Tel: 800-845-2292 (reservations) Tel: 970-725-3456
Fax: 970-725-3611
*Contact: Ken / Randy Sue Foscha*

**Open June to mid Sept.** • Western pack trips • 1 day pack trips + stays at ranch • Oct. to Nov. – hunts – mule deer, elk • Outcamp cabin available • Licensed Col. Outfitter # 277 – Call ranch for more information. See page 106.

Outfitters

## SOUTHFORK STABLES & OUTFITTERS, INC.

28481 Hwy. 160, Box WWRV Durango, CO 81301
Tel: 970-259-4871 Fax: 970-259-6996
*Contact: Rick / Kim Baird*
Licensed CO outfitters # 775

**Open April to Sept.** • 40 quarter horses • Western tack • Capacity 8 • Adults 15 years and older • All skill levels • 3 to 5 day cattle round up (optional team penning clinics) and customized pack trips • San Juan Nat'l Forest – Weimunuche Wilderness Waterproof range tipis • Heated cooking tent • Solar showers • Fall – elk, mule deer and bear hunting • Tent camps • Member: American Quarter Horse Assoc, CO Outfitters & Guide Assoc.

**Guest Ranch / Dude**

## DIAMOND D RANCH

PO Box 1555–WW, Boise, ID 83701
Tel: 800-222-1269 Tel/Fax: 208-336-9772 Call first
*Contact: Tom / Linda Demorest*

**Open June 1 to Oct. 15** • Western tack • 45 horses • Mountain trail horses • 3 to 7 day pack trips • Trail Riding • Swimming • Fishing • Hiking • Gold Panning • Hot tub • Volleyball • Horseshoes • Guest capacity of 35 • Member: Idaho Outfitters & Guide Assoc., Idaho Guest & Dude Ranch Assoc.

Situated in the Frank Church Wilderness Area, 40 miles north of Stanley, the ranch sits in a beautiful and remote valley – surrounded by millions of wilderness acres and abundant wildlife. The Demorest family have owned and operated the ranch for more than 45 years. We offer 3 to 7 day pack trips into spectacular mountains on sure-footed horses. Guests also vacation at the ranch where they may enjoy trailrides, gold panning, hiking, swimming, fishing in our creeks or lake, volleyball, horseshoes and photography, all in a week's stay. After a stretch in the saddle you'll want to ease back and enjoy evenings in the hot tub or sauna, or sharing stories around the campfire.

**Guest Ranch / Dude**

## HIDDEN CREEK RANCH

7600 East Blue Road, Harrison, ID 83833
Tel: 800-446-DUDE(3833) Tel: 208-689-3209 Fax: 208-689-9115
E Mail: hiddencreek@hiddencreek
Home Page: http//www.nidlink.com/~hiddencreek
*Contact: Laurie McKnight*

**Open May to Nov.** • Western tack • 75 horses • Mixed breeds – Quarter, Appaloosa, Paint, Morgan, Arab • 2 day 1 night pack trip June to Aug. • Average saddle time 6 to 8 hours • All skill levels • Gymkhana • Lessons • Mountain Riding • Guest capacity of 40 • Special children's program – June to Aug. • Special activities for adults only – trail riding, seven course candlelight dinner, pipe and sweat lodge ceremonies • Hot tubs • Fishing • Shooting • Mountain Bikes • Activities based in Native American Philosophy • Member: Dude Ranchers' Assoc., Idaho Guest and Dude Ranchers Assoc.

In a private valley surrounded by National Forests, experience an adventure vacation that celebrates life and generates joy and excitement. Daily scenic, challenging and fast rides – experienced riders welcome. Fish, trap-shoot, bike, boat tours, archery, gold mine and medicine-trail hikes. Stay in luxurious log cabins, eat gourmet meals and relax in hot tubs. Evening activities, seven-course candlelight dinner and quick draw contest. European attention to detail, first class accommodations and beautiful Idaho landscape. With a huge variety of activities, unparalleled horseback riding and unique, outstanding children's programs, Hidden Creek Ranch will leave you with memories of a great vacation that will last a lifetime.

Guest Ranch / Dude

## IDAHO ROCKY MOUNTAIN RANCH

HC 64 PO Box 9934, Stanley, ID 83278
Tel: 208-774-3544 Fax: 208-774-3477
*Contact: Reservations*

**Open June 8 to Sept. 16** • Western tack • 50 horses • Quarter horses • All skill levels • 1 to 10 day pack trips • Hot springs fed swimming pool • Hiking • Mountain biking • Nearby whitewater rafting, canoeing, kayaking • Fishing • Member: ID Outfitters & Guide Assoc., Property on National Historic Registry

Opened as a private guest ranch in the 1930s, the ranch now invites vacationers to come for a variety of fun activities, special outings, great meals, a western barbecue cookout and a spectacular view of the Sawtooth Mountains. On horseback, follow trails on the ranch or take rides in the Sawtooth and White Cloud Mountains. Soak in the hot springs swimming pool. Plan some whitewater rafting, canoeing, windsurfing, kayaking, or fishing. Venture out on a hike, enjoy mountain biking and rock climbing or visit a ghost town and other area attractions. It's a delightful place for visits in the uncrowded and scenic region.

Guest Ranch / Dude

## WAPITI MEADOW RANCH

HC 72, Dept WWRV, Cascade, ID 83611
Tel: 208-382-3217 Tel: 208-382-4336 (Radio-Phone)
Fax: 208-382-3217
*Contact: Diana Swift*

**Open May 1 to Oct. 31** • Western tack • 30 horses • Quarter horses and Crosses • Individually designed trail riding programs • Pack trips – 1 to 6 days • Up to 6 hours saddle time • All skill levels • Fall Hunting season – deer, elk • Fly fishing • Fishing • Hot tub • Guest capacity 12 to 14 • Member: Dude Ranchers' Assoc., Orvis Endorsed Fly Fishing Lodge, Idaho Guest & Dude Ranch Assoc., Idaho Outfitters & Guide Assoc.

Nestled in a lush, high mountain meadow where wild elk and deer graze among the horses, Wapiti Meadow offers riders, looking for comfort and fine dining, a wilderness adventure as well. From gentle valley paths to challenging summit tracks, endless miles of trail lead to sparkling lakes. Wind along crystal clear trout streams and top out on ridges with spectacular views of the mighty Northwest Rockies. Abundant wild game, excellent Orvis Endorsed trout fishing, gold-panning and secluded relaxation compliment the unlimited riding with individual guides and a different trail every day. Overnight and pack trips available by special arrangement.

**Outfitter**

## MYSTIC SADDLE RANCH

Fisher Creek Rd., WWRV, Stanley, ID 83278
Tel: 208-774-3591 Fax: 208-774-3455
*Contact: Deb or Jeff*

**Open June 1 to Sept. 30** • Western tack • 100 head • Daily trail rides • 5 day pack and customized trips • All skill levels • Combo pack – white water rafting • Hunting season – Oct. 15 to Nov. 9 – elk, mule deer • Fly fishing with instruction on trip into Salmon River – cutthroat, rainbow and dolly varden • Children over 6 • Member: Idaho Guides & Outfitter Assoc. • Licensed for Wilderness

Mystic Saddle Ranch has been offering quality wilderness trips into the rugged Sawtooth Range for more than 25 years. Let us show you high mountain peaks, glacial canyons, cobalt blue lakes and meadows where wildflowers abound and help you catch a wily trout. Young children and inexperienced riders feel comfortable on our gentle horses. Our trained guides are there to help you enjoy your wilderness surroundings. Come join us for this escape into a world of peaceful solitude, a time to relax the body and heal the soul while you experience the pristine beauty of this unique part of the world.

**Outfitter**

## RENSHAW OUTFITTING INC.

PO Box 1165, WWRV, Kamiah, ID 83536
Tel: 208-926-4520 Tel: 800-452-2567 Fax: 208-935-0788
*Contact: Jim Renshaw*

**Open July through August for pack trips** • Western tack • 20 saddle horses • Customized 7 to 10 day pack trips in Selway Bitterroot wilderness area • 4 to 5 hours a day riding • Limit to 10 riders • All skill levels • Fishing • Big game hunting • Clearwater Nat. Forest – May – black bear – Sept. – archery, elk – Oct. – rifle, elk • Deluxe base camps • Member: Idaho Outfitters & Guide Assoc.

Looking for that true getaway? Come and go with the best and most experienced outfitter in Idaho. Join us during the months of July and August for a progressive pack trip into the Selway Bitterroot Wilderness Area. In addition to the wonderful riding opportunities and beautiful scenery, there is excellent high mountain lake fishing. We also feature fishing trips to our deluxe tent camp at Weitas creek in June and August with its superb fishing opportunity for native cutthroat and rainbow trout. We offer big game hunting in the Clearwater National Forest including spring and fall hunts for black bear, elk hunts by archery and rifle in September and October respectively.

Bed and Breakfast

## SPECKLED MOUNTAIN RANCH

RR 2, Box 717, Bethel, ME 04217
Tel: 207-836-2908
*Contact: Susie Dixon / Leo Joost*

**Open May to Oct. for riding, B & B open all year** • English tack • Offer special 2 and 5 day riding packages, half day and all day rides • Summer riding camp for July • 9 horses • Haflingers, Morgans, Arabians, Quarter and 1 Mustang • Ride capacity of 4 • Guest capacity of 7 or 8 • All skill levels • Bordering White Mountain Forest • 3-1/2 hours from Boston, less than 2 hours from Portland

Come explore miles of beautiful mountain scenery on horses who enjoy their jobs. Whether you are interested in learning to ride, brushing up on skills or heading out on a vigorous all-day ride, we have packages to suit beginner through advanced. We sometimes go bareback for even more fun and adventure. We offer Intermediate and Advanced Summer Camp during the month of July for girls ages 11 to 15. For non-riding companions, there are miles of hiking trails and scenic dirt roads for biking enthusiasts, as well as bird watching, canoeing and many other outdoor activities nearby. Also enjoy fresh, healthy home-cooked meals.

Cattle Drives

## MONTANA HIGH COUNTRY CATTLE DRIVE

669 Flynn Lane, Townsend, MT 59644
Tel: 800-345-9423 Tel: 406-266-3612 Fax: 406-266-5306
Web: HTTP://WWW.IIGI.COM/OS/MONTANA/CATTLEDR/CATTLEDR.HTM
*Contact: Kelly / Ted Flynn*

**Drives in June and July** • Western tack • 60 Western Ranch horses • 6 hours in saddle a day • All skill levels • Guest capacity of 40 • Wagon transport for non-riders • Children 12 and older • Base camps – wagon supported • Fishing • Wildlife viewing • Hands-on natural education • Campfire session of western lore • Cowboy poetry, music • Member: Montana Outfitters & Guides Assoc., Mt. Stockgrowers Assoc.

Join us for an adventure you will remember for a lifetime! Montana High Country Cattle Drive takes you over routes followed for centuries by Indians, trappers, prospectors and ranchers to the rich green grass of the mountains. We are ten lifetime ranchers and licensed professional outfitters who want to share our western heritage and beautiful high country with you. Come join us as we take the cattle from our valley ranches to summer pastures in the mountains. Enjoy great riding, spectacular country and abundant wildlife while you do your part in getting the cattle to the mountains.

Guest Ranch / Cattle

## BONANZA CREEK COUNTRY

Lennep Rte. Box WWRV, Martinsdale, MT 59053
Tel: 800-476-6045 Tel/Fax: 406-572-3366
*Contact: June Voldseth*

**Open June, July and Aug.** • Western tack • 18 Quarter horses • 2 rides each day – 1 all day ride • Dinner steak out ride • Rides divided by skill level • Capacity 12 • 3, 4 and 7 day packages • Children older than 6 can ride with group • Baby sitting and corral riding for young ones • Camping • Lake swimming • Trout fishing • Mountain bikes • Fall hunting – Sept. through Nov. • Member: Montana Big Sky Ranch Assoc.

Since the 1870s, cowboys have worked cattle along Bonanza Creek. A century later, we've set the table for you. Bonanza Creek Country is a Montana cattle and guest ranch set in the legendary Crazy Mountains of south-central Montana. Relax in new log cabins and enjoy delicious home-cooked meals in the lodge. Ride as a small group through meadows, along streams, into the mountains or to the Indian pictographs, or help us gather cattle. Unlimited riding. Also great trout fishing, hiking, biking, wildlife watching and an overnight pack trip. An authentic ranch geared to those who prefer individual attention, comfort and a good time.

**Guest Ranch / Cattle**

## HARGRAVE CATTLE & GUEST RANCH

300 Thompson River, Marion, MT 59925
Tel/Fax: 406-858-2284
*Contact: Ellen*

**Open all year** • Western tack • 35 horses • Ranch horses • Unlimited riding opportunities • Cattle work all year • Cattle drives/roundups • 6 day pack trips • Hunting in season • All skill levels • Lessons • Guest capacity 15 • Special children's program – July and Aug. • Swimming • Stream fishing • Canoeing • 4W Drives • Shooting • Archery • Winter – cross-country and nearby downhill skiing • B&B opportunities • Member: MT Outfitters Assoc., Dude Ranchers' Assoc., National Cattleman

Hargrave's is a rare opportunity to really live the West. The 87,000 acre ranch heads a broad mountain valley of tall pines. It is an actual working cattle ranch with year round opportunities to join the crew. There's spring newborn calves, branding parties, summer cattle drives and fall roundups. A small guest list means individual attention on the trail or at the dining table. Summer brings overnight camps, herd and ridge top riding, canoeing the lakes nearby and trout fishing the river. Spring, summer and fall finds you sharing new friends around the fire or practicing your skeet shooting skills. Glacier National Park is a spectacular outing any month. Guests stay in "Headquarters" or cabins ranging from rustic to plush. Down comforters standard for all.

*See Color Photo Page 119*

**Guest Ranch / Dude**

## LAKE UPSATA GUEST RANCH

PO Box 6, WWRV, Ovando, MT 59854
Tel: 406-793-5890 Tel: 800-594-7687 Fax: 406-793-5894
Home page: www. upsata.com E Mail: jwgp@aol.com
*Contact: Richard Howe*

**Open May to Oct.** • Western tack • 30 + horses • Lessons • Guest capacity of 35 • Fly fishing • Special children's program • Wildlife programs • Swimming • Shooting • Tubing • Kayaks • Canoes

Lake Upsata Guest Ranch is located on a spectacular mountain lake in Western Montana and offers a truly unique recreational and educational experience for families and couples. There's something for everyone. We offer first class accommodations, hearty meals, fly fishing instruction on The Big Blackfoot River, horseback riding, wildlife programs and children's programs. There's also swimming, canoeing, boating, kayaking, hiking, tubing down the river, mountain biking, photography and much more. The programs are designed for all ages and abilities. For more information call 800-594-7686 or e-mail to: jwgp@aol.com. Visit our home page at www.upsata.com.

**Guest Ranch / Cattle**

## LONESOME SPUR GUEST RANCH

RR1, Box 110, Bridger, MT 59014
Tel/Fax: 406-662-3460
*Contact: Darlene Schwend*

**Open April 15 to Nov. 1** • Western tack • 16 Ranch horses • Trail riding • Team penning • Trail drives • Lessons (special professional lessons available) • All skill levels • Gymkhana • Trips to historical city of Cody, Red Lodge and Pryor Mountain Wild Horse Range • Rodeos • Guest Capacity of 10

Visit the Schwends on their 5th generation working cattle ranch in the shadows of Montana's Beartooth Mountains. Guests are invited to join our family and take part in ranching activities as the seasons demand, whether on the range trailing cattle, relaxing back at the ranch watching beautiful sunsets, mule and whitetail deer, the fleeting sight of a red fox or being awakened by the howl of a den of coyote pups. Accommodations include 2 Indian Teepees, 2 rooms in the ranch house bunk house and two log cabins. Close by the Yellowstone National Park and Custer Battlefield.

**Outfitter**

## A LAZY H OUTFITTERS

PO Box 729, Dept. CT, Choteau, MT 59422
Tel: 406-466-5564 Tel: 800-893-1155
*Contact: Sally Haas*

**Open July 1 to Sept 1** • Western tack • 20 horses • Tennessee Walkers, Quarter horses, Paints • 7, 8, 10 day trips • 5 hrs. a day riding • Capacity of 12 • Fly fishing (trout) • Hiking • Bob Marshall Wilderness and Chinese Wall • Sept. 15 thru Nov. – Hunting trips • Elk, mule deer, bear • Member: Montana Outfitters & Guide Assoc., Professional Wilderness Outfitters Assoc.

The Bob Marshall Wilderness is the second largest wilderness area in the continental US. We provide trips which emphasize different primary activities including fishing, riding, hiking and sight seeing. The travel days are filled with adventures as we travel from campsite to campsite, seeing new and exciting country. On days when we don't travel you may go on a short ride, hike, fish the trout filled streams or just lounge around camp.

**Outfitter**

## GREAT DIVIDE GUIDING AND OUTFITTERS

PO Box 315, Dept. WWRV, East Glacier Park, MT 59434
Tel: 800-421-9687 Tel/Fax: 406-226-4487
*Contact: Richard Jackson*

**Open June to Sept.** • Western tack • 25 horses • Quarter horses, ranch geldings • 5 day combination pack trip, cattle drive, horse drive • Limit 10 to a ride • All skill levels • Fishing • Member: Montana Outfitters & Guide Assoc., Professional Wilderness Outfitters Assoc.

Enjoy the rugged beauty of Glacier National Park without the crowd! Five day horse pack trips every Monday through Friday mid June through August. Spectacular scenery, well trained horses and high quality tack combine to make this an excellent adventure. Tent camps complete with comfortable sleeping pads and shower for your comfort and convenience are included. Enjoy unlimited riding, great trout fishing, swimming and exploring. Dutch oven apple pie, grilled steaks or chicken await you along with cowboy poetry and guitar for campfire entertainment under a star filled sky. During the week guests also help in a high country cattle roundup and a horse drive on the last day. One of Montana's premier outfitters since 1980.

**Outfitter**

## MONTE'S GUIDING & MOUNTAIN OUTFITTING

16 North Fork Rd. W., Townsend, MT 59644
Tel: 406-266-3515 Fax: 406-266-4026
*Contact: Monte Schnur*

**Open May through Nov.** • Western tack • 15 Western mountain horses • 1, 3, 5 day and customized pack trips – May through Aug. • Average saddle time 4 to 6 hours • Sept. through Nov. hunting trips – deer, antelope, bighorn sheep, bear and mountain lion • Spring float trips • Fishing • Member: Montana Outfitters & Guides Assoc.

Besides being a beautiful place, our area is home to some of the most abundant wildlife populations in Montana. We enjoy a mix of environments ranging from alpine mountains to dry plains and a lush river valley. If you enjoy nature, western lifestyle and history, you'll find it here! The country you'll ride over isn't much different today than it was when the Indian tribes hunted here. Whether you prefer to ride like the wind across meadows or let your horse pick his way over mountain trails, you'll have an unforgettable horseback adventure with us. Our full service trips are supported by an experienced staff.

**Outfitter**

## WHITE TAIL RANCH OUTFITTERS, INC.

Ovando, Mt. 59854
Tel/Fax: 406-793-5666
*Contact: Jack / Karen Hooker*

**Open May to Nov.** • Western tack • 50 horses, 40 mules • Saddle horses • All skill levels • Ranch stays • 10 day pack trips • 10 guests • Base camp and guided hunts, Sept. to Nov.• Elk, Mt. goat, black bear, grouse, white tail • Fishing • Member: Montana Outfitters & Guide Assoc.

Our philosophy is that despite our 50 years of experience, we are only as good as our last trip. Join us for fantastic rides in the Bob Marshall Wilderness where you will experience pristine wilderness, streams you can drink from, great fishing and a staff that knows how to get it right for all members of the family. We can customize the trips for your family's needs. Our hunting includes private licensed land, base camp drop off and guided pack hunts into the some of the most isolated mountain ranges. Please call or write for free brochures.

**Outfitter**

## WOLFPACK OUTFITTERS

Box 472, WWRV
Ennis, MT 59729
Tel: 406-682-4827
*Contact: Jeff Wingard*

**Open June through Dec.** • Western tack • 12 horses • Customized summer pack trips in Beaverhead Nat'l Forest • 1 to 7 day pack trips • 4 to 8 hours in saddle each day • All skill levels • Half and full day trail rides • Fall elk hunts • Archery – rifle • Heated tent base camps • Private land hunts • Member: Montana Outfitters & Guide Assoc. Lic. # 1799 Lee Metcalf Wilderness

**Guest Ranch / Cattle**

## N BAR RANCH / OUTLAW LAND & CATTLE CO.

PO Box 409, Dept. WWRV, Reserve, NM 87830
Tel/Fax: 505-533-6253 Tel/Fax: 800-616-0434
E mail: Ranchfun@aol.com
*Contact: Maile or Preston Bates*

**Open May through Oct.** • Western tack • 40 Quarter horses • Ranch vacations • Cattle drives/round-ups • Pack Trips – 7 and 10 days Gila wilderness • Team penning, roping • Specials – all women's week, kids week • Swimming • Hot tub • Fishing • Member: New Mexico Outfitters & Guide Assoc.

The N-Bar Ranch is a working cattle and horse ranch located high in the mountains of western New Mexico. We are not a dude ranch — we don't pamper. What we do offer is a chance to explore more than 100,000 acres of breathtaking high country on the back of one of the finest mounts this side of the Mississippi. Join us for a pack trip down the Gila River, where Geronimo was born, or take part in a real old-time round up and cattle drive, or become an outlaw for a week trying to elude a ruthless and persistent posse. Come see for yourself what it's all about. Tall pines, rolling grasslands, steep canyons, infinite wildflowers and a friendly staff.

**Outfitter**

## U-TRAIL – THE GILA WILDERNESS

Hwy. 180 & San Francisco River, PO Box 66
Glenwood, NM 88039-0066
Tel: 800-U-TRAIL-3 Tel: 505-539-2425 Fax: 505-539-2426
*Contact: Jim Mater, Kathy Atkinson*

**Open all year** • Western tack • 20 horses and mules • 6 to 8 day rides , 2 and 3 day specials • Progressive and base camp trips • All skill levels • 6 hours average time in saddle • Ride limited to 8 • Children welcome • Fishing • Natural hot springs on trail • Facility for client's horses • Member: New Mexico Guide & Outfitters

The Gila Wilderness... America's hidden treasure, located in southwest New Mexico. Breathtaking canyons, remarkable vistas, clear clean streams, abundant wildlife and few people all make a ride through the Gila Wilderness a lifetime experience. Natural hot springs and ancient Indian cliff dwellings add to the uniqueness of America's largest national forest. Birthplace of Geronimo. Ride surefooted horses and mules on progressive or base camp pack trips. Enjoy good company and good food. A ride you'll appreciate and forever remember. For intermediate to advanced riders we offer a high adventure trail ride. We pack light and ride far — please inquire.

**Inn**

## BARK EATER INN

PO Box 139 – CT, Alstead Hill Rd.,
Keene, NY 12942
Tel: 518-576-2221 Fax: 518-576-2071
*Contact: Reservations*

**Open all year** • English or Western tack • Thoroughbreds, Quarter horses, mixed breeds • All skill levels for trail riding • Polo • Riding lessons • Polo lessons • Complete riding packages • Winter program includes cross-country skiing • Minutes from Olympic Trail Complex • Guest capacity of 35

The inn is on an old farm, nestled in the Adirondack Mountains, minutes from the Winter Olympic Village of Lake Placid and connected by trails to the Olympic Trails cross-country complex. The inn offers a quiet, relaxed atmosphere with graciously appointed rooms and fine country gourmet meals. In the summer, the inn offers an extensive riding program, including polo. The stable has horses for both English and Western style riding. The experienced rider will enjoy the well trained, responsive horses. The beginner will be able to relax and gain confidence. Lessons, including polo, are available. Riding packages are designed to keep the price down and allow for lots of additional riding.

USA / NO

**Outfitter**

## COLD RIVER RANCH

Rt 3, Coreys, Dept. W, Tupper Lake, NY 12986
Tel: 518-359-7559
*Contact: John / Marie Fontana*

**Open all year** • Western tack • Riding mid May to mid Oct. • 15 Trail horses • 1, 2 and 3 day trail riding stays at Cold River Ranch • 2 and 3 night overnight wilderness pack trips – 6 to a trip • Average saddle time of 5 hours • All skill levels • Guest capacity of 10 • Canoeing • Hiking • Fishing • Facilities for clients' horses

For more than 25 years, the Cold River Ranch has helped outdoor people enjoy the Adirondack Wilderness area on horseback. Whether a person decides to venture on an overnight pack trip or ride locally and return to the Ranch in late afternoon, it is an outdoor experience. At the ranch or in pack camps we serve delicious, hearty meals. Our horses are gentle, well broken, sure-footed trail horses assigned to riders according to their weight and ability. On overnight rides, everything is supplied including sleeping bags with removable liners and saddle bags for your personal articles. Hunters accommodated in season at Ranch or Hunting Camp.

**Guest Ranch / Cattle**

## BADLANDS TRAIL RIDE

HCR 1, Box 64 WWRV, Killdeer, ND 58640
Tel: 701-764-5219
*Contact: Lynell Sandvick*

**Open spring, summer, fall** (year round possibilities) • Western tack • 25 Quarter horses • Camping • Cabins • Singles, couples, families, youth groups • All skill levels • Riding schedule to fit guests • Up to 6 hours a day in saddle

Experience the West That Was. Local ranch family offers western horseback riding experiences on thousands of acres of scenic Little Missouri River badlands. This unbelievably beautiful area is abundant with wildlife as well as beef cattle, Texas longhorns and horses. All kinds of camping and hand-crafted log cabins are available at nearby Eastview campground. This wooded area provides visitors with incredible seclusion and panoramic views. The cabins have electricity, padded sleeping platforms, tables and chairs. Outside there are fire rings, picnic tables and deck areas Camp and ride packages will be designed to fit guests' schedules and interests.

**Guest Ranch / Dude**

## BAKER'S BAR M RANCH

58840 Bar M Lane, Adams, OR 97810-3003
Tel: 541-566-3381
*Contact: The Baker Family*

**Open April to Sept.** • Western tack • 50 horses • Saddle horses • 2 rides daily, all day lunch rides and overnight campout (weather permitting) • All skill levels • Trout fishing (rainbows) • Pool • Square dancing • Birdwatching • Member: Dude Ranchers' Assoc.

For more than 50 years, the Baker Family has owned and operated the Bar M Ranch, developing it into one of the most unique and rewarding guest ranches in the West. The hand-hewn ranch house was built in 1864 and still serves as the heart of the Ranch for home-cooked meals and lodging. Horses are a big part of the Bar M, where a horse is picked to suit your riding skills, and it's yours for the week. The Ranch is located in the beautiful Blue Mountains of Eastern Oregon along the Umatilla River, 30 miles east of Pendleton. Please call or write the Bar M Ranch for more information.

**Guest Ranch / Cattle – Self Catering**

## OBSTINATE J RANCH

29680 Hwy.62, Trail, Oregon 97541
Tel: 541-878-2718 Fax: 541-878-4389
*Contact: Martha Brooks*

**Open all year** • English and Western tack • 15 grade horses • Quarter, Appaloosa and Mixed breeds • Trail riding • Arena riding • Cattle work • Cattle Drives • Dressage • Jumping • Lessons • All skill levels • Hunting in season • Fishing trout, steelhead and salmon • Rafting • Hiking • Guest capacity 20 • Tennis • Swimming • Sauna • Recreation room • Shopping and restaurant nearby

A working horse and cattle ranch, located on the banks of southern Oregon's famous Rogue River, we are a rider's paradise. Offering English and Western, our rides are tailored to guests' levels of experience and cover the spectrum from spectacular trails rides to cross-country jumps and cattle drives. Guests can also enjoy fly and traditional fishing for the region's greatest trout, steelhead and salmon on our nearly full mile of private riverfront, as well as hiking, rafting and more. All guests stay in fully furnished guest houses with complete kitchens. Additional activities include the nearby Peter Britt Music Festival (Aug.), the Ashland Shakespearean Festival (Feb. and Oct.), scenic Crater Lake and Historic Jacksonville.

**Guest Ranch / Cattle**

## PONDEROSA CATTLE COMPANY

PO Box 190, Seneca, OR 97873
Tel: 800-331-1012 Tel/Fax: 503-542-2713
*Contact: Reservations*

**Open all year** • Western tack • Summer riding program May to Oct. • 100 horses • Quarter and grade • All skill levels • 18 and older • Guest capacity 48 • Fishing • Jacuzzi • Hunting in season • Hiking • Paved airstrip

The largest working guest ranch in the Northwest. Selected as one of the top 26 guest ranches by National Geographic Traveller. Set your cowboy spirit free in the wide open spaces of a 120,000 acre cattle ranch. Where a healthy ride, tending to 3,500 cattle, a cozy chat around a blazing fireplace in the rustic 7,000 sq. foot lodge and great food can remind you of how the West was won. Beautiful fauna, deer, elk, antelope, flocks of water fowl, eagles and other wildlife are common sights along with a staff that delights in serving you. By car – 6 hours from Portland, 3 hours from Redmond, Oregon, 4 hours from Boise. Air taxi service and Ponderosa Ranch Bus available for transfers.

**Outfitters**

## EAGLE CAP WILDERNESS PACK STATION

High Country Outfitters, Minam Lodge
59761 Wallowa Lake Hwy., Box WWRV, Joseph, OR 97846
Tel: 503-432-4145 Tel: 800-681-6222
Fax: 503-432-4145 (call first)
*Contact: Woody, Marlene, Matt and Marc McDowell*

**Open May through Dec.** • Sept. to Dec. hunt season • Western tack • 100 horses • Quarter, Paint, Appaloosa, Mules • All skill levels • Minam Lodge Capacity of 24 • Daily riding • Customized pack trip • Combination 6 to 10 day pack and river float trips • Hunting – elk, deer, bear, cougar, big horn sheep (with tag only), coyote • Fishing • Member: Oregon State Guides & Outfitters and Eastern Oregon Guides & Outfitters

Welcome to the spectacular Eagle Cap Wilderness, the largest wilderness in Oregon with 58 pristine high lakes and peaks that range from 3600 feet to 9845 feet. Also enjoy Hells Canyon, the deepest gorge in North America which hails the awesome Snake River. From our Wallowa Lake pack station we offer hourly, daily horseback rides, guided deluxe pack trips, drop camps or ride or fly in to our no-roads secluded wilderness. Minam Lodge offers tranquillity, good fishing and daily horseback riding, too. Call us to design for your family the trip of a lifetime.

**Bed & Breakfast / Bring your own horse**

## BUNKHOUSE BED & BREAKFAST

14630 Lower Spring Creek Road, Box WWRV  Hermosa, SD  57744
Tel:  605-342- 5462    Fax:  605-343-1916
*Contact:  Carol Hendrickson*

**Open May 1 through Dec. 31** • Bring your own horse • Intermediate to advanced skill required on trails in Black Hills, Custer State Park, Badlands Nat'l Park • Join cattle drives in season • Guided ride possibilities • Ride to Mt. Rushmore • Camping sites • Guest capacity in B&B is 10 • Member:  B&B Innkeepers of SD, Badland & Lakes Assoc.

Load up your favorite horse and come ride the beautiful Black Hills and Badlands of South Dakota. See Mt. Rushmore from the back of your horse, view 5 states from atop Harney Peak, ride where the outlaws hid out in the Badlands or through buffalo herds in Custer State Park. In the peaceful, quiet setting of our ranch you'll fall asleep to the sounds of the coyotes and the creek, awaken to the birds singing and our delicious "all you can eat" ranch breakfast prepared for a great day of riding. Spin tall tales over an evening campfire – relax, enjoy! Families welcome. Horses can be rented with guides nearby at reasonable prices.

**Outfitter**

## ALL 'ROUND RANCH

PO Box 153, Dept. WWRV, Jensen, UT 84035
Tel: 801-789-7626 Tel: 800-603-8069 Fax: 801-789-5902
*Contact: Wann Brown*

**Scheduled trips May to Sept.** • Western tack • 25 Quarter horses • 4 and 6 day or customized trips • Base camps • Instructional emphasis • Cowboy skills • Horsemanship • Guest capacity of 12 • Children 12 and older on family trip • Member: Utah Guides and Outfitters Assoc., America Outdoors

Not a "nose-to-tail ride." Emphasis on participation, instruction and lots of riding. Four or six-day small group, range riding/cowboy adventures on the panoramic rangeland flanking Dinosaur National Monument in Colorado. More than twenty years in adventure-based learning. Specialize in teaching cowboy horsemanship to the novice or experienced rider. You'll be paired with one of our quality, ranch-raised Quarter horses, selected to match your skill level. Cattle work included in the riding opportunities. Ride at all gaits in a variety of terrain. Camp out at working cattle camps. All gear provided.

**Outfitters**

## HONDOO RIVERS & TRAILS

PO Box 98, Torrey, UT 84775
Tel: 801-425-3519 Tel: 800-332-2696 Fax: 801-425-3548
E-Mail: hondoo@color-country.net
*Contact: Pat Kearney*

**Open May 1 to Nov. 1** • Western tack • 15 saddle horses • Quarter horses and Crosses • 3 to 6 day pack trips + customized • 10 person limit • Buffalo, big horn sheep and wild horse expeditions • Cattle roundups • 3 to 6 hrs. riding each day • 4 wheel vehicle trips • River trips – raft or kayak • Children 14 and older • Member: Utah Guides & Outfitters Assoc., Back Country Horsemen of Utah – Operate under permits from Capitol Reef Nat'l Park, USFS, BLM

Hondoo owners Gary George and Pat Kearney, unable to improve upon the incredible variation and beauty in Utah's canyon country, have designed more than 11 different riding trips to help you enjoy the experience. Their emphasis is on sharing with guests their extensive knowledge of the history, geography, geology, fauna and wildlife of the area. Special trips include separate wild horse, elk, antelope and buffalo expeditions. All their trips are owner led, supported by 4 wheel drive chuckwagons that bring you the unusual trail luxuries of sleeping pads, chairs, showers and ice. The extensive use of support vehicles allows experienced riders a good opportunity for paced riding where terrain permits.

**Outfitter**

## FLYING J OUTFITTERS

Box 284, Myton, Utah 84052
Tel: 801-646-3208
*Contact: Lawny Jackson*

**Open May to Nov.** • Western tack • 25 horses and mules • All skill levels • Base camps • Progressive pack trips • Customized trip length – 4 day minimum • 6 to 10 guests a trip • Photography trips • NE Utah (Bookcliff and Uintah mountains) • Member: UT Outfitters & Guides Assoc., Worldwide Outfitters & Guides Assoc.

**Outfiller**

## J/L OUTFITTER & GUIDES, INC.

PO Box 129, Dept. WWRV, Whiterocks, Utah 84085
Tel: 801-353-4049 Fax: 801-353-4181
*Contact: Joe / Linda Jessup*

**Open May through Oct.** • Western saddle • 25 Quarter horses • Saddle time unlimited • All skill levels • Lessons for beginners • 3 to 5 day pack trips with base camps • Small custom tailored groups • Owner operated • Ranch stays – log cabins with full kitchen and daily trail riding • Fishing • Hiking • Member: UT Guides & Outfitters Assoc.

**Inn to Inn / Stationary – Riding Clinic**

## KEDRON VALLEY STABLES

RT. 106, PO Box 368, South Woodstock, VT 05071
Tel: 802-457-1480 Tel: 800-225-6301 Fax: 802-457-3029
*Contact: Paul Kendall*

**Open all year** • Inn to inn riding mid May to mid Oct. • English tack • 40 horses • Half-Arabian, Quarter, Thoroughbred, Morgan • 5 night, 4 day Green Mountain Inn-to-Inn Ride • Intermediate to advanced skills • 2 night – 2 day Weekend Inn-to-Inn Ride • Adult Riding Clinic Stationary • All skill levels • Vehicle supported inn rides • Historic country inns • Excellent cuisine • Winter sleigh rides

For those so inclined, the Green Mountain Inn to Inn Ride is a delightful way to walk, trot and canter one's way through the Green Mountain State, boarding and dining at a select group of historic country inns. Riding distances average 20 to 25 miles a day. The trip is for intermediate and advanced riders with the leg capacity for up to six hours a day in the saddle. Riders pass beautiful summer estates, horse farms, newly mown fields, maple tree groves, stone walls and covered bridges, all within view of the Green Mountains. Also available on a year-round basis: hourly trail rides, lessons, boarding, training, carriage rides and sleigh rides.

**Inn to Inn**

## VERMONT ICELANDIC HORSE FARM

PO Box 577, Depart WWRV, Waitsfield, VT 05673
Tel: 802-496-7141 Fax: 802-496-5390
*Contact: Karen Winhold*

**Open all year** • English (Icelandic saddles) tack • Helmets provided • Rain gear can be provided • 25 Icelandic Horses • Half day and full day rides • All skill levels • 2 to 6 day inn to inn rides • Experience required • Skjoring • 8 riders maximum • Full service inn accommodations.

The Vermont Icelandic Horse Farm features guided inn to inn riding on smooth gaited Icelandic Horses. Trips vary from 2 to 6 days and guests stay at the finest inns of scenic Mad River Valley. The inns are charming, elegant and serve excellent cuisine. Informal attire prevails. The temperament of the Icelandic horse is steady and willing and their movements are unique. In addition to the common gaits of walk, trot and canter, they also possess the additional gaits of tolt and pace. The tolt is a smooth, four beat gait that enables the horse to cover rough terrain and long distances with swiftness, grace and ease. Winter riding is truly an unforgettable experience on what people say is the most comfortable riding horse in the world.

**Resort**

## MOUNTAIN TOP INN

Chittenden, VT 05737
Tel: 802-483-2311 Tel: 800-445-2100 Fax: 802-483-6373
*Contact: Douglas DiSabito*

**Open all year** • English and Western tack • 50 horses • Quarter, Thoroughbreds, Arabians • All skill levels • Lessons available • Hunter/jumper, dressage • Introductory polo • Trail riding • Fly fishing • Claybird shooting • Tennis • Golf • Beach and Lake Activities • Fine Dining

Everyone, from never-ridden-before beginners to advanced horsemen, will find what they're looking for at Mountain Top Inn. All riders can tailor personalized riding programs to their desires and ability levels, making them as varied and intensive as they wish. The 35-room inn is situated in the heart of central Vermont's Green Mountains and overlooks a spectacular pristine lake. In addition, Mountain Top has cottages and chalets to accommodate families and small groups. Known as "Vermont's Best Kept Secret," Mountain Top Inn offers the best of both worlds — an intimate country inn with numerous facilities, steeped in the finest New England tradition.

**Inn**

## THE CONYERS HOUSE INN & STABLE

3131 Slate Mills Road, Sperryville, VA 22740
Tel: 540-987-8025 Fax: 540-987-8709
*Contact: Sandra Cartwright-Brown*

**Open all year** • English tack • 8 horses – 3 hunters • Trail riding with instruction • All skill levels • Limit 5 guests a ride • Inn to inn ride by arrangement • Fox hunting • Cross country • Facility for horses • Guest Capacity 20 + • Fishing • Swimming • Hiking • Children 10 and older • Founding member: B&B Virginia

Located in the midst of Virginia's most beautiful hunt country, the Conyers House is nestled in the foothills of the Blue Ridge Mountains. Two hour trail rides through this magnificent scenery include instruction for novices. Advanced riders may hunt or hilltop with the world famous Rappahannock Hunt. Excellent hiking, fishing, shooting, antiquing, five star dining in the county, Civil War battlefields, Monticello, Skyline Drive, golf, tennis and swimming are nearby. The Conyers House offers 8 rooms all with private bathrooms, fireplaces, A/C and porches. A large delicious breakfast and refreshments in the afternoon are included. A seven course candlelit dinner is available by advanced reservation. ABC licensed. Pets and children accepted in certain rooms.

**Outfitter**

## VIRGINIA MOUNTAIN OUTFITTERS, INC.

c/o Deborah Sensabaugh
Rt. 1, Box 244, Buena Vista, VA 24416
Tel: 540-261-1910 Tel: 540-261-3841
*Contact: Deborah Sensabaugh*

**Open all year** • Western and English tack • 10 mountain horses and mules • All skill levels • Ride size limited to 6 people • Half and full day rides, Moonlight trail ride, Horse Lover weekend holiday, deluxe trail riders – 2 nights at Sugar Tree Inn, foxhunting weekends, five day inn to inn rides, customized pack trips, trout fishing trip, overnight camp outs • Accommodations at inns or camping • Twenty minutes from Lexington, Virginia – home of Virginia Horse Center • Swimming possible in season • Winter rides at lower elevations • Transfers can be arranged

We are a full service outfitter located in the Shenandoah Valley, near historic Lexington, Virginia and the beautiful Blue Ridge Mountains where we usually ride. Our trails are easy to moderate and generally mountain terrain prevails, keeping the ride at a slow pace for the safety of horse and rider. Where terrain permits and if desired, we do some trotting and cantering. We offer a wide variety of packages including inn based weekend rides from Lavender Hill Farm and deluxe two night packages from beautiful Sugar Tree Inn where a room with a whirlpool (if available) and masseuse awaits your weary bones. Camping trips can be arranged without difficulty in season.

**Outfitter**

## GRAY WOLF OUTFITTERS

PO Box 56, Dept. WWRV, Silverdale, WA 98383
Tel: 360-692-6455 Fax: 360-692-0986
*Contact: Glen Cantwell*

**Open April – Nov.** • Western tack • Mixed breeds and mules • All skill levels • Drop camps • 1/2 and 1 day rides, deluxe progressive pack trips – 2 to 6 days • Average saddle time 4 to 6 hours • Guest capacity 4 to 10 • Hunting trips – Sept 1. through December 15 – archery, muzzle loader, modern firearms – elk (Roosevelt), deer, bear and cougar (call or write for details) • Member: Washington Outfitters & Guide Assoc.

We are the western-most outfitter in the contiguous United States and the only one outfitting in the pristine Olympic National Park (also in Olympic National Forest) with mules and horses. Visit the rain forest on the Quinault or Hoh Rivers. Ride through the beautiful virgin old growth timber or the high alpine divides and see snowy mountains and glaciers such as Blue Glacier on Mount Olympus. While you ride, you have the opportunity to see Roosevelt elk, deer, mountain goats and bear. Nowhere else can you experience this and get in some fishing as well.

**Outfitter**

## NORTH CASCADE OUTFITTERS

PO Box 395 W, Twisp, WA 98856
Tel: 509-997-1015
*Contact: John P. Doran*

**Open June to Oct.** • Western tack • Experienced mountain horses • All skill levels • Children 8 and older welcome • Pack trips • Base camps • Day rides • Fall hunting trips • Fishing • Member: Washington Outfitters & Guide Assoc.

Join us for customized pack trips into the 500,000-acre Pasayten Wilderness area of the Northern Cascades. The scenery is spectacular and diverse from steep valleys and craggy peaks to peaceful high meadows brimming with wildflowers. Your trip can be planned to include excellent high mountain lake fishing for rainbow and cutthroat trout. In addition to our full service trips, we offer a full range of customized trips including walk and pack combinations and base camps. We also pack hunters for Early Buck and General Deer Hunting Seasons.

**Inn / Inn to Inn**

## SWIFT LEVEL

RR. 2, Box 296A, Lewisburg, West Virginia 24901
Tel: 304-645-1155 Fax: 304-647-5212
*Contact: Jimmy / Tootie O' Flaherty*

**April 1 to mid Nov.** • English tack • 50 horses • Thoroughbreds, Quarter horses, Connemara and Thoroughbred Cross • 5 day all inclusive inn to inn trips • Ride capacity 2 to 8 • Skill level intermediate • Riding programs from inn • Cross-country jumping • Mountain biking • White water rafting • Nearby sporting clays • Hiking • Canoeing • Caving • Skiing in season • Nearby therapeutic massage • Guest Capacity of 12 •

A beautiful 150 acre farm, built in the early 1820s, is situated in the heart of the lush Greenbrier Valley, nestled deep in the breath taking Allegheny Mountains of West Virginia. Ride through some of the most spectacular country in the United States on the famous O'Flaherty horses and Connemara ponies. We offer 1 to 5 day riding packages through hundreds of miles of trails, farms and centuries old roads. Enjoy Swift Level's excellent fresh food and lull to sleep in wonderful accommodations after an unforgettable day's ride. The area is rich in alternative activities including mountain biking, hiking, white water rafting and more. Direct air from NY, Wash., Pitt. and Charlotte to Lewisburg. Transfers from Lewisburg.

Cattle Drive

## LOZIER'S LONESOME DOVE CATTLE DRIVE

Box 100–WWRV, Cora, WY 82925
Tel: 800-822-8466 Tel: 307-367-4868 Fax: 307-367-6260
*Contact: Irv and Levi Lozier*

**Open May 25 to Sept. 15** • Western tack • 100 horses • Quarter horses and riding mules • Average saddle time 7 hours each day • All skill levels • Adult only (18+ years or 16 w/guardian) • Lessons available • Pack trips • Ranch stays • Cattle drives • Cattle roundups • Swimming • Fishing

Join the Lozier's (Adult Only) Lonesome Dove Cattle Drive for a week and live the life of a True Western Cowboy. Move 50 to 1000 cattle to summer mountain pastures and ride through unforgettably spectacular scenery. Camp on the trail for 3 days and enjoy the tranquillity and exceptional dutch-oven cooking. Learn to catch, tack, ride and care for your own personal horse like an everyday cowboy would. Learn how to punch cows efficiently, read brands, sort cattle, gather, "mother up" and identify sick cattle. All-inclusive weekly vacations for 16 participants, singles and couples welcome.

**Guest Ranch / Dude**

## BITTERROOT

PO Box 807, Dubois, WY 82513
Tel: 800-545-0019 Tel: 307-455-3363 Fax: 307-455-2354
*Contact: Reservations*

**Open late May through Sept.** • English and Western tack • 160 horses • Half of herd are purebred Arabian • Three horses per guest • Optional videotaped riding lessons • Course of 60 jumps for advanced riders only • Wilderness pack trips • Private fly fishing stream and stocked ponds • Individual log cabins • Main lodge with dining room, pool room, piano, library and sitting room • Member: Dude Ranchers' Assoc.

The Bitterroot Ranch has a strong riding program with three horses to a guest and excellent instruction. It is a good place to prepare for overseas trips and to improve riding skills. It is also an excellent place for those less keen on riding or for families to enjoy the magnificence of the Rockies in a remote setting 16 miles from the highway at the end of a valley bordering the National Forest. Fly fishing opportunities both on the ranch and nearby are some of the best and least crowded in the Rockies. There are plenty of places to hike and observe wildlife. Individual log cabins provide a maximum of comfort and privacy. The atmosphere is international and there are usually European guests.

**Guest Ranch / Dude**

## BLACKWATER CREEK RANCH

1516 Northfork Hwy., Cody, WY 82414
Tel: 307-587-5201
E mail: bwcranch@wave.park.wy.us
Web: http://www.wyo.net/blackwater
*Contact: Tom / Debbie Carlton*

**Open June through September** • Western tack • 60 horses • Quarter horses and mules • Daily scheduled rides and customized riding programs • Heated pool • 14 person hot tub • Billiards • Fly fishing • Hiking • White water rafting • Special children's program • Outdoor barbecues • Trips to Cody museums and rodeo • Trips to Yellowstone National Park • Member: Dude Ranchers' Assoc.

PHOTO: LAURA OSEREDZUK

Blackwater Creek Ranch offers a mountain dude ranch experience that is ideal for families with an interest in riding, special programs for the children, a full range of planned activities if desired and the ever present spectacular scenery along with abundant wildlife. We are located at 7,000 feet in the scenic river valley between Cody an Yellowstone at the intersection of Blackwater Creek and the North Fork of the Shoshone River. The riding occurs both in the creek and river area and in the Absaroka Mountains that surround our ranch. Riders are assigned horses for the week by the wranglers paying close attention to your needs and abilities. Children participate in special activities and join their parents at the weekly evening rodeo in Cody. Our heated pool, large hot tub and great fly fishing are ideal additions to our riding programs. Very comfortable, fully modernized 1930s built rustic cabins and extraordinary ranch food round out an unforgettable Western experience.

*See Color Photo Pages 120, 121 and Inside Front Cover*

**Guest Ranch / Cattle**

## BRETECHE CREEK RANCH

PO Box 596, Cody, WY 82414
Tel: 307-587-3844 Tel: 307-587-5067 Fax: 307-527-7032
*Contact: Reservations*

**Open June to mid Sept.** • Western tack • Guest capacity 20 • Rustic • Education combined with western recreation • Special sessions • Ornithology • Horsemanship clinics • Natural and cultural history • Swimming • Wood-fired hot tub • Fishing • Naturalist on staff • Tours of Yellowstone Nat'l Park and historic Cody • Gourmet food

Breteche Creek offers a unique educational vacation experience in a spectacular setting. As a 7,000 acre working cattle and horse ranch with frequent opportunities to wrangle horses, move cattle and take horsemanship classes, we combine the best of a traditional guest ranch with educational activities ranging from ornithology and astronomy to writing and photography. Rustic by design we have created a camplike atmosphere without electricity and phones (we do have hot showers and gourmet food). Guests stay in "tent cabins" scattered among the aspens along Breteche Creek. So come join us for our unique brand of high country mountain based camp retreats.

**Guest Ranch / Dude**

## DIAMOND L GUEST RANCH

PO Box 70 – WWRV, Hulett, WY 82720
Tel: 800-851-5909 Tel: 307-467-5236
Fax: 307-4677-5486 (Call first)
*Contact: Gary / Carolyn Luther*

**Open all year** • May to Oct. – traditional guest ranch • B & B rest of year • Western saddle • 24 Quarter horses • Several rides daily including all day rides • Small groups divided by skill level • Guest capacity 18 • Hot tub • Mountain Bikes • Family games • Campfires • Nearby golf, tennis, fishing • Winter – cross-country skiing and snowmobiling • Member: Assoc. Member Dude Ranchers' Assoc.

The original ranch was homesteaded in the late 1890s, located eighteen miles from Devil's Tower, the nations first national monument. It features a 4,000 square foot Cedar Log Lodge with three deluxe guest rooms that share two baths and a two unit cabin with private baths. Bring your appetite for great western home-cooked meals. A unique riding program geared for the individual guest that includes riding in the Wyoming Black Hills National Forest which borders the ranch on two sides. Enjoy a breakfast and supper ride. Also enjoy hiking, fishing, mountain biking, horseshoes, volleyball, indoor and outdoor games and campfires. Close to sightseeing in Wyoming and South Dakota.

**Guest Ranch / Dude**

## HALF MOON LAKE GUEST RANCH

PO Box 983, Pinedale, WY 82941
Tel: 307-367-6373 Tel: 208-788-9800 (Winter) Fax: 307-367-6538
*Contact: Frank Deede / Julia Ware*

**Open May to Nov. and Feb. and March** • Western tack • 30 mountain horses • Trail rides • Unlimited riding opportunities • 1 to 10 day guided pack trips • All skill levels • Fully guided big game hunts in season • Luxury wilderness camps • Ski-boat rentals • Fishing boats • Moorage • Hiking • Fishing • Lake swimming • Golf nearby • Winter cross country skiing, snowmobiling • Lakeside restaurant • Weddings • Seminars • Member: WY Outfitters & Guide Assoc.

The ranch lies in vast Bridger-Teton National Forest, among aspens and pines on the shore of Half Moon Lake. In the summer our program offers unlimited opportunities for guided rides in the endless wilderness as well as plenty of opportunity for fun on the lake, including fishing and water skiing. Rides range from a beautiful 2.5 hour loop around Half Moon lake to all day rides for great fishing and adventure. Many of our guests stay at Half Moon on the way to 1 to 10 day wilderness pack trips or as a beginning and end to their hunt into the wilderness area. Guests stay in comfortable individual log cabins.

**Guest Ranch / Cattle**

## HIGH ISLAND RANCH

PO Box 710, Depart. WRV, Hamilton Dome, WY 82427
Tel/Fax: 307-867-2374
*Contact: Karen Robbins*

**Open May through Sept.** • Western tack • 40 Quarter horses • All skill levels • Unlimited riding • 1800s cattle drive week • Branding and round-up weeks • High mountain fast riding adventure weeks • Guest capacity 25 • Trout Fishing • Special family weeks • Member: WY. Dude Ranchers Assoc.

Sign on, "cowhands," for High Island's 1800s Cattle Drive. Spend the week enjoying the "Old West" as you ride the range as cowboys have done for more than a century. Work as much or as little as you like while moving cattle on a 45 mile drive to seasonal grazing grounds. Enjoy hearty meals served out of an authentic chuck wagon and learn the lore of the West. Although it's a rustic setting, the cattle drive weeks, branding & round-up weeks, prairie to high mountain round-up weeks, trout fishing and high mountain riding adventure weeks offer the unbeatable luxury of spectacular vistas, great food, friendly people and adventure.

**Guest Ranch / Dude**

## LAZY L & B RANCH

1072 East Fork Rd – Box WWRV, Dubois, WY 82513
Tel: 800-453-9488 Tel: 307-455-2839 Fax: 307-455-2634
*Contact: The Naylons*

**Open end of May to mid Sept.** • Western tack • 60 Quarter horses • Rides divided by skill level • Supervised riding program for children 5 and older including 3 early meals a week followed by supervised activities • Solar heated pool • Fishing • Riflery • Cowboy poetry and song after dinner • Corral games, horseshoes, ping pong and pool • 35 to 40 person capacity • Sept. – adults only • Member: Dude Ranchers' Assoc., WY. Dude Ranchers Assoc.

The Lazy L & B Ranch is known for the quality of its riding program because of our experienced staff and the riding that takes you through a West you have never seen before. Blessed with an unusual variety of environments, from cottonwood river bottoms and red rock canyons to alpine mountain meadows, we are a rider's paradise. You are assigned your own horse for the week. Riding groups never exceed seven and are divided by skill level. Whether you ride or not, you can take a hike, fish or relax in our solar heated pool. Enjoy home style meals, BBQs and picnics with fresh breads and desserts daily. The cabins and lodge offer casual western comfort.

**Guest Ranch / Cattle**

## LOZIER'S BOX R RANCH

Box 100-WWRV, Cora, WY 82925
Tel: 307-367-4868 Tel: 800-822-8466 Fax: 307-367-6260
*Contact: Levi Lozier*

**Open May 25 to Sept.15** • Western tack • Family weeks • Adults only weeks • 100 quarter horses and mules • Guest capacity 20 • Beginners welcome • Lessons available • Swimming • Fishing • Also offer 3 to 10 day Pack trips • Cattle drives • Wagon trips • Member: WY Outfitters & Guide Assoc.

Join the Lozier's 100 year old tradition at the finest working cattle/horse guest ranch in Northwest Wyoming, just 60 miles from Jackson Hole, Teton and Yellowstone Parks. All inclusive adult only, family or group weeks planned. Spring/Fall cattle drives with 100 to 1000 cattle. Secluded mountain valley bordering the 840,000 acre Bridger National Forest. Enjoy your own personal horse with freedoms not found elsewhere.

**Guest Ranch / Dude**

## PARADISE GUEST RANCH

PO Box 790,WWRV, Buffalo, Wy 82834
Tel: 307-684-7876 Fax: 307-684-9054
*Contact: Susan / Leah*

**Open May 20 thru Oct. 1** • Western tack • 130 horses • Quarters, TB, Appaloosa, Crossbreeds • All skill levels • Pack trips • Special children's programs – kid's rodeo, some babysitting services • Sept 1 – 22 adults only • Heated swimming pool • Hot tub • Fishing • Nearby golf, tennis • Guest capacity 70 • Member: Dude Ranchers' Association

A traditional guest ranch in the Big Horn Mountains that keeps its ear to the ground as to what today's guests want such as half day and all day rides with or without kids. One wrangler to seven guests ratio. Pack trips are available. Deluxe log cabins, fireplace, porch, kitchenette and living room help to make your wilderness adventure very comfortable. Great fishing and a fishing guide can provide many delightful hours of relaxation and good eating. Singalong bonfire, talent night, kids overnight, chuckwagon dinner, square dance, swim pool, hot tub, hikes and kids rodeo are some of the activities we offer in a place we call Paradise.

**Guest Ranch / Dude**

## RIMROCK RANCH

2728 Northfork Route, Depart CT, Cody, WY 82414
Tel: 307-587-3970 Fax: 307-527-5014
*Contact: Gary / Dede Fales*

**Open June 1 through Sept.** • Western tack • 120 trail horses • Rider assigned a horse for ranch stay • Riding small groups • Weekly ranch gymkhana • Lessons available • 4 to 8 day pack trips • Guest capacity 32 • Fishing • Lake and river swimming • Recreation room with pool table • Member: Dude Ranchers' Assoc.

The Fales family has been operating Rimrock Ranch for more than forty years and through two generations and they take great pride in providing what can only be called a seven day Western happening. After a day of getting settled and meeting the "folks," you will be introduced to the horse that is exclusively yours for the week with instruction offered where needed. There will be plenty of rides divided by skill and fitness level. There are frequent cookouts before, in the middle of and after rides. Guests are taken to Cody Night Rodeo for one evening. There are ranch softball games, a river float, cowboy singing, all day rides for the willing, a full day escorted tour of Yellowstone Park and more. Guests sleep in comfortable cabins.

Guest Ranch / Cattle

## SANDY GAP RANCH

**Let's Gallop Horseback Adventures**

PO Box 1486, Pinedale, WY 82941
Tel: 307-367-6700 Tel: 307-360-8650 (Mobile)
*Contact: Frank Deede / Julia Ware*

**Open April 15 to Nov. 15** • Western tack • 20 quarter horses • Intermediate skill level required • Average riding time 5 to 7 hours a day • Daily cattle gathering • Spring branding • Fall roundups • Roping and cutting lessons • Special 3 night – 2 day **Cowboy Quickies** • Bunkhouse accommodations • 2 bedroom cabin • Guest capacity is 20 • Fishing • 90 mile semi-annual horse drives • Transfers from Jackson Hole • Member: WY Outfitters & Guide Assoc.

We are an authentic cattle ranch on a 200,000 acre grazing association. Riding time on our quality horses is spent assisting the association's cowboys move. Doctor and work with 2,000 cows. The country is open and wild and the Wind River Range is always in view. The ranch is remote and rustic. The accommodations are comfortable and hearty ranch fare is served family style. Spring branding and big country fall roundups are always a lot of fun. Get a roping or cutting lesson from one of our knowledgeable wranglers with decades of cowboy experience. The roping arena is equipped with rolling practice steer and a video camera. Please ask about our semi-annual 90 mile horse drives.

**Guest Ranch / Dude**

## 7 D RANCH

PO Box 100, Depart WWRV, Cody, WY 82414
Tel/Fax: 307-587-9885 (office) Tel: 307-587-3997 (Ranch)
E mail: ranch7d@Wyoming.com
*Contact: Ward and Nikki Dominick*

**Open June 1 to Sept. 15 (summer season)** • Open Dec. through Feb. (winter season) • Western tack • 65 horses • Quarter horse types • 2 rides each day except Sunday • 8 riders to a group divided by skill levels and preference • Up to 8 day customized pack trips into surrounding wilderness and Yellowstone backcountry • Gymkhana • Fall hunts • Fishing • Trap-shooting • Hiking • Bird watching • Square Dances • Special children's program • Winter – Cross-country skiing • Member: Dude Ranchers' Assoc.

The Dominick family has offered guest vacations at the Seven D Ranch since 1959. Today, as the old West quickly disappears, the Seven D still offers unbeatable hiking, fishing, horseback riding, pack trips and photographic opportunities. We are surrounded by the North Absaroka Wilderness. Yellowstone National Park is 1-1/2 hours away by car. Morning and afternoon rides vary in length and skill level. Excellent horses, great instructors, brunch rides and all day rides are available. After a day's outing, followed by a sumptuous meal served family-style, guests can relax in their own private cabin, participate in an evening event or just tell stories 'round the campfire.

**Guest Ranch / Cattle**

## THREE QUARTER CIRCLE RANCH

PO Box 243 – CT, Lander, WY 82520
Tel: 307-332-2995 Fax: 307-332-7902
*Contact: Jim Allen*

**Open May 15 to Oct. 15** • Western tack • 30 ranch raised Quarter horses • Intermediate skill level required • Cutting, reining, roping • 6 hours a day in saddle • Guest capacity 6 to 8 • Fishing • Member: WY Farm Bureau & Stockgrowers Assoc. • Free pick up and drop off at the Riverton, WY airport

Ride to your heart's content on Wyoming's splendid Three Quarter Circle Ranch, a 35,000 acre working cattle ranch! Not a dude ranch, this week long cowboy experience will leave you tired and saddlesore – but wanting more. We run 1,000 cows over vast, empty rangelands, just like our pioneering ancestors did. You may become part of the cowboy crew, trailing cattle, branding and roping, as well as learning western ranch riding fundamentals like cutting and reining. Neighbors still help neighbors out in this part of the West. Send for free information.

**Outfitter**

## ALL AMERICAN OUTFITTERS

PO Box 745, WWRV, Wilson, WY 83014
Tel: 307-733-9434 Tel: 800-452-3831 (outside WY)
*Contact: Forest Stearns*

**Open mid June through Nov.** • Mid-June through mid-Sept. 6 day and customized pack trips • Western tack • 30 horses • Mountain horses and riding mules • Average saddle time 3 to 8 hours • Groups of 2 to 10 • Lake and stream fishing for cutthroat, brook, rainbow and golden • Fall hunting season – Trophy Elk, Big Horn Sheep • Base camps – limit of 6 • Member: WY Outfitters & Guide Assoc. – Outfitters License # 9; Insured

Having been born and raised in the mountain ranges outside of Jackson Hole, we love sharing our knowledge and wilderness experience with friends and clients. Our mid June to September pack trips through the Teton Wilderness and the Shoshone National Forest are perfect for families and small groups interested in gentle horses and mules, great river, stream and lake fishing, photography and wilderness appreciation. Our pack trips are all customized and full service. Our fall guided hunts are from comfortable western style wilderness base camps that we pack into. By limiting our group to 6 we are able to insure the highest quality service. Our success ratio over the last 10 years speaks for itself.

Outfitter

## GARY FALES OUTFITTING

2768 Northfork Route, Cody, WY 82414
Tel: 307-587-3747 Fax: 307-527-5014
*Contact: Gary / Dede Fales*

**Open June 1 through Sept.** • Summer pack trips 4 to 8 days • All skill levels • Average saddle time 4 hours • 100 + horses • Mountain trail horses and pack animals • Guest capacity 6 to 8 • Deluxe 5-person tents for couples • Foam pads • Fishing • Sept. to Dec. – hunting – elk, deer, antelope, moose and sheep

Twenty years of experience, sure-footed riding horses and government permits to pack into Yellowstone National Park as well as Bridger-Teton and Shoshone National Forests mean our fellow packers are in for a great wilderness experience. The fishing can be downright exhilarating with the Yellowstone cutthroat an aggressively feeding, hard fighting fish which we expect to cook for breakfast or dinner. We pay strict attention to "light on land" camping techniques. Photographic and sightseeing opportunities also are available! Our fall hunting program offers deluxe base camps and privately guided hunts.

**Outfitter**

## GREEN RIVER OUTFITTERS

PO Box 727, Pinedale, WY 82941
Tel: 307-367-2416
*Contact: Bill Webb*

**Open May 1 to Sept. 31** • Western tack • Mixed breed – experienced mountain horses – Quarter horses • Daily rides • Overnighters • 5, 7 and 10 day pack trips • Base camps at Rim Buck Wilderness Lodge • Daily horse roundup • All skill levels • Lessons available • Fishing trips • Photography trips • Guided float trips • Member: WY Outfitters Assoc.

Our trips begin at Rim Buck Lodge, built by trappers in 1900 and located in Bridger-Teton National Forest. Cabin or walled tents offer comfortable sleeping arrangements. Some folks like to arrange their trip from this comfortable base camp and ride out daily, fish, hike, pan for gold or simply relax. We offer structured 3 and 5 day holidays from this camp with guided rides and good opportunities for wilderness photography. One overnight in a wilderness camp is included in the 5 day trip. We also offer a 7 and 10 day progressive pack trip into the Gros Ventre Wilderness Area. All our trips provide good food, cooks, tents, wranglers, experienced mountain horses and transportation from Jackson Hole.

**Point to Point / Campsite to campsite**

## OREGON-PONY EXPRESS TRAIL ADVENTURE

Let's Gallop Horseback Adventures
PO Box 1486, Pinedale, WY 82941
Tel: 307-367-6700
*Contact: Frank Deede / Julie Ware*

**Open May through Oct.** • Western tack • 25 horses • Quarter horses • Fit and competent riders • Vehicle supported • Comfortable base style camps with showers, chairs • 5 to 10 day program • 4 to 15 riders • Average saddle time is 5 hours a day • Ride ends at Sandy Gap Ranch • Member: WY Outfitters & Guide Assoc.

Enjoy our 7 day west central Wyoming journey on the Oregon-Pony Express Trail made famous by the first western settlers and the US Mail carrying Pony Express riders. We ride through 120 miles of high desert, alpine vistas and rugged, challenging terrain. The trip concludes at our ranch located at the foot of the spectacular Wind River mountains. We provide well trained seasoned Quarter horses matched to your riding ability. The ride is supported by staff and vehicle and we offer tall tents, chairs, showers and deliciously prepared meals. Participants can expect to see wildlife in their habitat, improve their horsemanship and experience the real wild west.

# Therapeutic Horseback Riding for Individuals with Disabilities

Saddling up on a horse is an enjoyable experience for many people, but for an individual with a disability it can signify much more – a road to recovery. Each year people with physical, cognitive and emotional disabilities benefit from therapeutic horseback activities. Research shows that individuals of all ages who participate in therapeutic riding can experience physical, emotional and mental rewards. Because horseback riding gently and rhythmically moves the rider's body in a manner similar to a human gait, riders with physical disabilities often show improvement in flexibility, balance and muscle strength. For individuals with mental or emotional disabilities, the unique relationship formed with the horse can lead to increased confidence, patience and self-esteem. The sense of independence found on horseback benefits all who ride.

Since 1969, the North American Riding for the Handicapped Association (NARHA) has promoted and supported therapeutic horseback riding programs throughout the United States and Canada. At some 500 centers, more than 26,000 individuals with disabilities benefit from equine-facilitated activities.

To learn more about therapeutic riding, contact one of the following associations:

North American Riding for the Handicapped Association
PO Box 33150, Denver, CO  80233
USA Tel:  800-369-7433    Tel: 303-452-1212

Riding for the Disabled Association International
Wootton Hall, New Milton, Hampshire BH25 5SJ,  England

Kuratorium fur Therpapeutisches
Reiten E.V. , Bundesgeschaftsstelle, Freiherr von Langen strass, 13,
4410 Warendorf 1, Germany

Riding for the Disabled Association of Australia
First Floor, 1 Cookson St.,
Camberwell, Victoria 3124, Australia

# Wild Horse Inmate Program (WHIP)

WHIP is a self supporting, cost efficient program which is labor intensive and educates inmates in skills such as equine management and horse training while instilling good work ethics.

This allows WHIP to supply an affordable trained horse to the general public and also helps the Bureau of Land Management place wild horses in good homes.

The Mustang has legendary traits of being sure-footed, possessing great endurance and being an "easy keeper." These animals have sturdy legs and rarely suffer the leg and tendon problems so common among the more domesticated varieties of horses. This gives the wild horse the ability to perform with ease in all types of terrain. The Mustang is a superior trail or pack horse and is excellent at any endeavor in which a rider needs a horse that "won't give up when the going gets tough." Trained Mustangs have a quick mind and an honest nature.

Under the expert supervisions of WHIP supervisor Tony Bainbridge, the horses are trained in a humane and safe way for horse and trainer. The horse's natural instincts and behavior are used to help the Mustang willingly accept the training process. The proof of Bainbridge's wisdom and patience is that the horses from this program involving intensive inmate labor are in strong demand.

For more information about adoptions and free training seminars call OR WRITE W.H.I.P. supervisor Tony Bainbridge .

Tel: 719-269-4500

Fax: 719-275-2850

Write to: JUNIPER VALLEY PRODUCTS<br>PO BOX 1600,<br>CANON, CO 81215-1600

# Travel Services

**EQUITOUR LTD.**
PO Box 807, Dubois, WY 82513, USA
Tel: 800-545-0019 Tel: 307-455-3363 Fax: 307-455-2354
E mail: equitour@Wyoming.com
*See back cover and pages 4, 172, 192*

**EQUITREK AUSTRALIA**
5 King Road, Ingleside NSW 2101
Tel: (61)-2-9913-9408 Fax: (61)-2-9970- 6303
E mail: equitrek@magna.com.au
Web Page: http://www.equineoz.com.au/equitrek
*See color photo page 116 and pages 16, 17, 18, 21–28*

**FITS EQUESTRIAN**
685 Lateen Road, Solvang, CA 93463
Tel: 805-688-9494 Fax: 805-688-2943
*See page 10*

**HIDDEN TREASURES OF ITALY**
934 Elmwood Ave., Wilmette, Illinois 60091
Tel: 847-853-1312 Fax: 847-853-1340
E mail: htreasure@aol.com
*See pages 56–60*

**IBUSZ INTERNATIONAL, AMERICAN TRAVEL ABROAD**
250 W. 57th St., NYC, NY 10107 USA
Tel: 212-586-5230 Tel: 1-800-367-7878 Fax: 212-581-7925
*See page 51*

**PEGASUS REITERREISEN (RIDING VACATIONS)**
Grenzacherstr 34
CH-4058 Basel, Switzerland
Tel: (41)-61-693-0485 Fax: (41)-61-691-2093
*See color photo pages 114 and 115*

**WORLDWIDE ORGANIZATION OF EQUESTRIAN TOURISM**
**ORGANIZACION MUNDIAL DE TURISMO ECUESTRE**
C / Floranes 60, 39010 Santander, Spain (Espana)
Tel: 942 -37 - 3321 Fax: 942-37-3321 (Numbers within Spain)
From US dial 011-34-4237-3321
*See pages 41, 63, 66–68, 193*

# Equitour

PO Box 807, Dubois, WY 82513
Tel: 800-545-0019 (Outside WY)
Tel: 307-455-3363 (In WY-International) Fax: 307-455-2354
E mail: equitour@wyoming.com

## Equitour's Worldwide Riding Holidays

Equitour organizes riding holidays in the United States and 30 other countries, but we are not just tour operators – we are also horse people. For more than 25 years we have been leading rides from our own Wyoming ranch, Bitterroot, where we have 160 horses and raise and train purebred Arabians. Equitour holidays are for adventurous people who are prepared to break with routine and discover new places and experiences in partnership with a good horse. Our role is to offer a broad spectrum of the top rides in the world which best suit the interests and abilities of our clients. We do this by monitoring the performance of our outfitters, by sending our own people and our associates with them and by the feedback we get from clients, each of whom is asked to fill out a questionnaire about various aspects of the ride. We are constantly on the lookout for new trips and spend a great deal of time investigating those with the best potential.

One of our greatest advantages is that we ride with 500 or so people at our own ranch each year and this gives us a good chance to evaluate their reactions on the spot. Their comments on other rides they have taken become more meaningful as we see how they handle our own horses under different conditions. It gives us a better idea of how to offer what they are really seeking. We are able to give people lessons in the most effective techniques to use so that the partnership between horse and rider works to the highest advantage and enjoyment.

Please call or write for our color catalogue featuring more than 100 riding possibilities. Please call or write for a copy and then talk to one of our ride consultants about the most appropriate choice for you.

# Worldwide Organization of Equestrian Tourism (O.M.T.E.)

## Organizacion Mundial de Turismo Ecuestre

The Worldwide Organization of Equestrian Tourism (O.M.T.E.) is a non-profit entity founded in 1990 for the purpose of promoting equestrian tourism at a worldwide level. It has already established a worldwide network of membership and it has particularly strong representation in the Spanish speaking countries and Europe.

The philosophy of the organization is that the promoting of riding vacations depends not only on promotional efforts of the suppliers but also on the quality of the businesses offering those excursions. As a result, members of O.M.T.E. must comply with strict norms covering infrastructure, facilities, horses and established routes for riding.

In addition to its promotional efforts, the O.M.T.E. provides legal assistance, veterinary advice and operates a school for equestrian guides in Jaca, Spain. Each member of the organization must have a representative accredited by the school in Jaca.

For more information and reservations, contact the main headquarters at the following address:

Organizacion Mundial de Turismo Ecuestre
C / Floranes 60
39010 Santander, Spain (Espana)
Tel: 942-37-3321 Fax: 942-37-3321 (Numbers within Spain)
From US dial 011-34-4237-3321

## SOME SPECIAL CATEGORIES



## AUTHOR'S NOTES

* Bring your own horse – Many places allow it, I listed only one place that specializes.

** Endurance as a specialty – There are many other rides requiring fit and competent or advanced riders and fit and competent horses.

English and Western style riding is now worldwide. Please note that stock saddles, calvary saddles, all resemble western type saddles. Ireland, Italy and Spain offer Western but conversely many places in the United States offer English style riding.

Mule riding is mentioned in book. You might want to try it – a lot of people like them critters.

## Hunting/Fishing

Nearly every North American outfitter, many ranches and some "overseas" outfitters and properties offer hunting and fishing opportunities.

Hunting is a seasonal activity and follows the dictates of individual states' and countries' hunting laws and licenses. In North America, the season is usually the fall. As a rule, suppliers of horse vacations are reluctant to list their hunting operations out of respect for those who see hunting as cruel and unusual punishment. In fairness to their positions, let me add that the author, as a non-hunter, saw no indication of anything but the utmost respect for wildlife and the land it lives on. If there is a fight between those who want to develop the land and those who love its undeveloped wilderness, it is surely not coming from those who make their living off the preservation of the wilderness.

## Shooting

Sport shooting of non living objects can be conducted safely at many of the wilderness ranches under the careful standards the ranches set. For those of you interested in that sport, an inquiry at many of the places listed in the book may bring a positive response despite the absence of shooting as a listed activity.

## INDEX BY PAGE NUMBER / CONTINENT/ COUNTRY / REGION / SKILL LEVEL / SEASONS / BASIC CLASSIFICATION (TYPE/SPECIALITY)

| PAGE | CONTINENT COUNTRY REGION | RIDE | SKILL | SEASONS | TYPE SPECIALTY |
|---|---|---|---|---|---|
| 29–35 | **NEW ZEALAND** | | | | |
| 30 | North Island | Pakiri Beach Horse Rides | ASL | All year | Point to P Farm stays |
| 31 | North Island | Te Urewara Adventures | ASL | All year | Point to P Camp. / Plus |
| 32 | North Island | Whananaki Trail Rides | ASL | All year | Point to P Farmhouse |
| 333 | South Island | Kohwai Equest. | Farm Stay | ASL | All year Farm stay |
| 34 | South Island | Back-Country Saddle Exp. | ASL | All year | Point to P Camp. / Plus |
| 35 | South Island | Western Ranges Horse Treks | ASL | All year | Self catering Point to P |
| 37–43 | **CARIBBEAN, CENTRAL AND SOUTH AMERICA** | | | | |
| 38–39 | **CARIBBEAN** | | | | |
| 38 | **Dominican Republic** | Casa de Campo | ASL | All year | Resort |
| 39 | **Jamaica** | Chukka Cove Farm, LTD. | ASL | All year | Res. R. C. |
| 40–42 | **CENTRAL AMERICA** | | | | |
| 40 | **Belize** | Banana Bank Lodge | ASL | All year | Resort Treks |
| 41 | **Costa Rica** | Welcome to Costa Rica | ASL | All year | Country Hotels |
| 42 | **Mexico** | Rancho Madrona | ASL | All year | Guest Ranch |
| 43 | **SOUTH AMERICA** | | | | |
| 43 | **Ecuador** | Andes High Mt. Adventure | ASL | All year | Country house + |
| 45–73 | **EUROPE** | | | | |
| 46–49 | **France** | | | | |
| 46 | Ile De France | Ferme Ecuestre de la Folie Panier | ASL | All year | Point to P Cottage |
| 47 | Normandy | Le Harras de la Perfide Albion | ASL | All year | Farmhouse |
| 48 | Provence | Provence-Trail | Advan. | March to Nov. | Point to P |
| 49 | Touraine | Ferme de Launay | Int. | All year | B&B |
| 50 | **Greece** | Hippocampus Farm | ASL Fit/C | March to Nov. | Point to P Farmhouse |
| 51 | **Hungary** | Hortobagy Tour | Int. | April to Oct. | Point to P |
| 52–54 | **Ireland** | | | | |
| 52 | Co. Kerry | El Rancho Horse Holidays, LTD. | Int. | May to Sept. | Point to P |
| 53 | Co. Mayo | Clew Bay Trail & Drummindoo RC | ASL | All year | Point to P Res. R. C. |
| 54 | Co. Tipperary | Ballycormac House | ASL | All year | Guest House |

| Page | Continent Country Region | Ride | Skill | Seasons | Type Specialty |
|---|---|---|---|---|---|
| 55–60 | **Italy** | | | | |
| 56 | Tuscany | Antico Casale di Scansano | Int. | March to Jan. | Inn |
| 57 | Tuscany | Il Paretaio | ASL | All year | Inn<br>Res. R.C. |
| 58 | Umbria | Azienda Malvarina | Int. | All year | Point to P |
| 59 | Umbria | La Casella | Int. | March to Jan. | Res. R.C. |
| 61 | **Norway** | Fjellrittet | Int. | June to Aug. | Point to P |
| 62 | **Portugal** | Hotel Rural A Coutado | Int. and Adv. | All year | Res. R.C., Hotel |
| 63–68 | **Spain** | | | | |
| 63 | Andalusia | Cabalgar Rutas Alterativas | Int. | All year | Point to P |
| 64 | Andalusia | Finca La Mota | Int. | All year | Inn |
| 65 | Andalusia | Hurricane Hotel | ASL Int. | All year | Hotel<br>Point to P |
| 66 | Basque Country | Rutas A Caballo Turismo Artziniega | Int. + | All year | Point to P |
| 67 | Majorca | Escola D'Equitacio Son Menut | ASL | Sept.-May<br>All year | Point to P<br>Trail riding |
| 68 | Tarragona | Hipica Delta | ASL | Sept to June<br>All year | Point to P |
| 69–73 | **UNITED KINGDOM** | | | | |
| 69 | **England** | Exmoor Riding Holidays | Advan. | Apr. to Nov. | Point to P |
| 70–71 | **Scotland** | | | | |
| 70 | **Scotland** | Hayfield | ASL | All year | Res. R.C. |
| 71 | **Scotland** | Highland Icelandic Horse Trekking | Int. | March to Oct. | Point to P |
| 72–73 | **Wales** | | | | |
| 72 | Dyfed | Cae Lago | ASL | March to Nov. | Farmhouse<br>Point to P |
| 73 | Gwent | Grange Trekking Centre | ASL | March to Nov. | Point to P<br>Farmhouse |
| 74–188 | **NORTH AMERICA** | | | | |
| 75–83 | **Canada** | | | | |
| 75 | Alberta | Black Cat Guest Ranch | ASL | All year | Guest Ranch<br>Dude |
| 76 | Alberta | Alberta Frontier Guiding / Outfitting | ASL | All year | Outfitter |
| 76 | Alberta | Horseback Adventure, LTD | ASL | June to Sept. | Outfitter |
| 77 | Alberta | Holiday on Horseback | ASL | May to Oct. | Outfitter |

| PAGE | CONTINENT COUNTRY REGION | RIDE | SKILL | SEASONS | TYPE SPECIALTY |
|---|---|---|---|---|---|
| 78 | British Columbia | Big Bar Guest Ranch | ASL | May to Sept. | Guest Ranch Dude |
| 79 | British Columbia | Circle H Mountain lodge | ASL | | Guest Ranch Dude |
| 80 | British Columbia | Three Bar Cattle and Guest Ranch | ASL | All year | Guest Ranch Dude |
| 81 | Quebec | Au Jal A Cheval | ASL | May to Oct. | Point to P |
| 82 | Quebec | La Ferme du Joual Vair | ASL | May to Nov. | Point to P |
| 83 | Quebec | Ranch Massif du Sud | ASL | All year | Point to P Res. R. C. |
| 84–188 | **United States** | | | | |
| 84 | Alaska | Majestic Mt. Alaskan Adven. Inc. | ASL | June to Aug. | Lodge Outfitter |
| 85 | Alaska | Northland Ranch Resort | ASL | May to Nov. | Guest Ranch Cattle |
| 86 | Alaska | Wolf Point Ranch | ASL | June to Aug Feb. to April | Outfitter Dog sled/ snowmobiling |
| 87 | Arizona | Grapevine Canyon Ranch | ASL | All year | Guest Ranch Cattle |
| 88–89 | Arizona | Horseshoe Ranch on Bloody Basin Rd. | Int. | All year | Guest Ranch Cattle |
| 90 | Arizona | Kay El Bar Ranch | ASL | Oct. to May | Guest Ranch Dude |
| 91 | Arizona | Lazy K Bar Ranch | ASL | All year | Guest Ranch Dude |
| 92 | Arizona | White Stallion Ranch | ASL | Oct to May | Guest Ranch Dude |
| 93 | Arizona | Don Donnelly Horseback Vac. | ASL | Mar. to Nov. | Outfitter |
| 94–95 | California | Howard Creek Ranch | ASL | All year | Inn |
| 96 | California | Hunewill Guest Ranch | ASL | May to Oct. | Guest Ranch Cattle |
| 97 | California | McGee Creek Pack Station | ASL | May to Sept. | Outfitter Cattle/ Wagons |
| 98 | California | Lari Shea's Ricochet Ridge Ranch | ASL | All year | Point to point /RRC. |
| 99 | California | Adventures on Horseback | Int. | April to Oct. ASL | Res. RC |
| 100 | California | Alisal Guest Ranch & Resort | ASL | All year | Resort |
| 101 | Colorado | Kirkwell Cattle Company | ASL | May to Oct. | Cattle Drives |
| 102 | Colorado | Bar Lazy J Guest Ranch | ASL | May to Oct. | Guest Ranch Dude |

| PAGE | CONTINENT COUNTRY REGION | RIDE | SKILL | SEASONS | TYPE SPECIALTY |
|---|---|---|---|---|---|
| 103 | Colorado | C Lazy U Ranch | ASL | May to Oct. Dec.– March | Guest Ranch Dude |
| 104 | Colorado | Colorado Guest Ranch/ Chipeta R | ASL | All year | Guest Ranch Cattle |
| 103 | Colorado | Colorado Ranch Connection, Inc | ASL | June to Sept. | Guest Ranch Cattle |
| 105 | Colorado | Colorado Trails Ranch | ASL | June to Sept. | Guest Ranch Dude |
| 106, 132 | Colorado | Drowsy Water | Ranch ASL | June to Sept. | Guest Ranch Dude/Outfitter |
| 103 | Colorado | Harmel's Guest Ranch | ASL | May to Sept. | Guest Ranch Dude |
| 107–108 | Colorado | Wit's End Guest and Resort Ranch | ASL | May to Oct. | Guest Ranch Resort |
| 109 | Colorado | Capitol Peak Outfitters | ASL | May to Sept. | Outfitter |
| 110 | Colorado | Double Diamond | ASL | All year | Outfitter |
| 111 | Colorado | Drowsy Water Ranch | ASL | June to Sept. | Outfitter Ranch |
| 111 | Colorado | Marvine and Lunney Outfitters | ASL | May to Nov. | Outfitter |
| 112 | Colorado | Rapp Guides & Packers | ASL | All year | Outfitter |
| 128 | Colorado | Red Feather Guides/ Outfitters | ASL | May to Oct. | Outfitter |
| 129 | Colorado | San Juan Outfitting, LLC. | ASL | April to Nov. | Outfitter |
| 130–131 | Colorado | Fox Equestrian | ASL | May to Oct. | Cross-Country Res. R. C. |
| 132 | Colorado | Southfork Stables & Outfitters,Inc. | ASL | April to Sept. | Outfitter |
| 133 | Idaho | Diamond D Ranch | ASL | June to Oct. | Guest Ranch Dude |
| 134 | Idaho | Hidden Creek Ranch | ASL | May to Nov. | Guest Ranch Dude |
| 135 | Idaho | Idaho Rocky Mountain Ranch | ASL | June to Sept. | Guest Ranch Dude |
| 136 | Idaho | Wapiti Meadow Ranch | ASL | May to Oct. | Guest Ranch Dude |
| 137 | Idaho | Mystic Saddle Ranch | ASL | June to Sept. | Outfitter |
| 138 | Idaho | Renshaw Outfitting Inc. | ASL | July to Oct. | Outfitter |
| 139 | Maine | Speckled Mountain Ranch | ASL | May to Oct. | B&B |
| 140 | Montana | Montana High Country Cattle Dr | ASL | June/July | Cattle Drives |

| Page | Continent Country Region | Ride | Skill | Seasons | Type Specialty |
|---|---|---|---|---|---|
| 141 | Montana | Bonanza Creek Ranch | ASL | June to Aug | Guest Ranch Cattle |
| 142 | Montana | Hargrave Cattle & Guest Ranch | ASL | All year | Guest Ranch Cattle |
| 143 | Montana | Lake Upsata Guest Ranch | ASL | May to Oct. | Guest Ranch Dude |
| 144 | Montana | Lonesome Spur Guest Ranch | ASL | Apr. to Nov. | Guest Ranch Cattle |
| 145 | Montana | A Lazy H Outfitters | ASL | July to Nov. | Outfitter |
| 146 | Montana | Great Divide Guiding/Outfit. | ASL | June to Sept. | Outfitter |
| 147 | Montana | Monte's Guiding & Mt. Outfitting | ASL | May to Nov. | Outfitter |
| 148 | Montana | White Tail Ranch Outfitters, Inc. | ASL | May to Nov. | Outfitter |
| 149 | Montana | Wolfpack Outfitters | ASL | June to Dec. | Outfitter |
| 150 | New Mexico | N Bar Ranch / Outlaw Cattle Co. | ASL | May to Oct. | Guest Ranch Cattle |
| 151 | New Mexico | U-Trail - The Gila Wilderness | ASL | All year | Outfitter |
| 152 | New York | Bark Eater Inn | ASL | All year | Inn |
| 153 | New York | Cold River Ranch | ASL | All year | Outfitter |
| 154 | North Dakota | Badlands Trail Ride | ASL | All year | Guest Ranch Cattle |
| 155 | Oregon | Baker's Bar M Ranch | ASL | Apr. to Sept. | Guest Ranch Dude |
| 156 | Oregon | Obstinate J Ranch | ASL | All year | Guest ranch Cattle |
| 157 | Oregon | Ponderosa Cattle Company | ASL | All year | Guest Ranch Cattle |
| 158 | Oregon | Eagle Cap Wilderness Pack Station | ASL | May to Dec. | Outfitter |
| 159 | South Dakota | Bunkhouse Bed & Breakfast | Int. | May to Dec. | Bring your own horse |
| 160 | Utah | All 'Round Ranch | ASL | May to Sept. | Outfitter |
| 162 | Utah | Flying J Outfitters | ASL | May to Nov. | Outfitter |
| 161 | Utah | Hondoo Rivers & Trails | ASL | May to Nov. | Outfitter |
| 162 | Utah | J/L Outfitter & Guides, Inc. | ASL | May to Oct. | Outfitter |
| 163 | Vermont | Kedron Valley Stables | Int. ASL | All year | Inn to Inn Res. RC |
| 164 | Vermont | Vermont Icelandic Horse Farm | Int. ASL | All year | Inn to Inn |

| PAGE | CONTINENT COUNTRY REGION | RIDE | SKILL | SEASONS | TYPE SPECIALTY |
|---|---|---|---|---|---|
| 165 | Vermont | Mountain Top Inn | ASL | All year | Resort |
| 166 | Virginia | The Conyers House Inn /Stable | ASL | All year | Inn |
| 167 | Virginia | Virginia Mountain Outfit. | ASL | All year | Outfitter |
| 168 | Washington | Gray Wolf Outfitters | ASL | Apr. to Nov.. | Outfitter |
| 169 | Washington | North Cascade Outfitters | ASL | June to Oct. | Outfitter |
| 170 | West Virginia | Swift Level | Inter. | Apr. to Nov | Inn Inn to Inn |
| 171 | Wyoming | Lozier's Lonesome Dove Cattle Drive. | ASL | May to Sept. | Cattle Drive |
| 172 | Wyoming | Bitterroot | ASL | May to Sept. | Guest Ranch Dude |
| 173 | Wyoming | Blackwater Creek Ranch | ASL | June to Sept. | Guest Ranch Dude |
| 174 | Wyoming | Breteche Creek Ranch | ASL | June to Sept. | Guest Ranch Cattle |
| 175 | Wyoming | Diamond L Guest Ranch | ASL | All year | Guest Ranch Dude |
| 176 | Wyoming | Half Moon Lake Guest Ranch | ASL | May-Nov. Feb-March | Guest Ranch Dude |
| 177 | Wyoming | High Island Ranch | ASL | May to Sept. | Guest Ranch Cattle |
| 178 | Wyoming | Lazy L & B Ranch | ASL | May to Sept. | Guest Ranch Dude |
| 179 | Wyoming | Lozier's Box R Ranch | ASL | May to Sept. | Guest Ranch Cattle |
| 180 | Wyoming | Paradise Guest Ranch | ASL | May to Oct. | Guest Ranch Dude |
| 181 | Wyoming | Rimrock Ranch | ASL | June to Sept. | Guest Ranch Dude |
| 182 | Wyoming | Sandy Gap Ranch | Inter. | Apr. to Nov. | Guest Ranch Cattle |
| 183 | Wyoming | 7 D Ranch | ASL | June to Sept. | Guest Ranch Dude |
| 184 | Wyoming | Three Quarter Circle Ranch | Int. | May to Oct. | Guest Ranch Cattle |
| 185 | Wyoming | All American Outfitters | ASL | May to Nov. | Outfitter |
| 186 | Wyoming | Gary Fales Outfitting | ASL | June to Dec. | Outfitter |
| 187 | Wyoming | Green River Outfitters | ASL | May to Sept. | Outfitter |
| 188 | Wyoming | Oregon-Pony Express Trail Adv | Fit/C | May to Oct | Point to P Camping |

ASL = All skill levels  Fit / C = Fit and competent  Int. = Intermediate
Point to P = Point to Point  Adv. = Advanced

To purchase additional copies of Worldwide Riding Vacations, please send $14.00 U.S., plus $3.00* for cost of shipping and handling to:

The Compleat Traveller
2425 Edge Hill Road
Huntingdon Valley, PA 19006
USA

Books may be ordered with Discover, Master, or Visa cards at:

Tel: 215-659-3281
Fax: 215-659-9347
E mail: csacks@voicenet.com

Look for current and updated material on our website on
Horsenet (see opposite cover)
http://www.horsenet.com/compleat

Comments on the book, reviews of places and suggestions are welcome and should be sent to the above address, Depart. CT.

* $20.00 Canadian plus $5.00 Canadian for shipping.

---

**Payment Method**

❑ VISA — Quantity________ Price Each ____________

❑ MasterCard

❑ Check or Money Order — Shipping & Handling ____________

❑ Discover — Total Price ____________

Credit Card Number ____________________________________________

Expiration Date ____________________________________________

Signature ____________________________________________

*Shipping Address – No P.O. Boxes for UPS shipments (Please Type or Print)*

Name ____________________________________________

Organization ____________________________________________

Address ____________________________________________

City ________________________________ State ____________________

Zip ________________ +4 ____________ Country ____________________